BODY ART TATTOO DESIGNS

- **Henna Designs**
- **Tribal**
- **Floral**
- **Celtic**
- **Astrology**
- **Names**
- **Bands**
- **Tiny Tattoos**

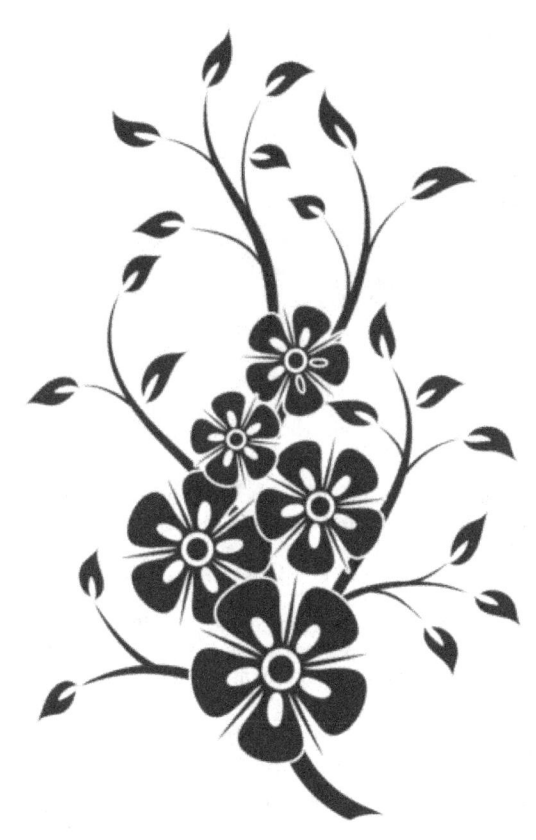

Over 800 designs including birth names and inspirational wording.

Copyright © 2020 by T. Irvolino
All rights reserved. No part of this book may be used or reproduced or transmitted in any form or   by any means, electronic or mechanical including photocopying, recording, or by any information storage or retrieval system without express written permission from the publisher.

The information provided within this Book is for general informational purposes only. While we try to keep the information up-to-date and correct, there are no representations or warranties, express or implied, about the completeness, accuracy, reliability, suitability or availability with respect to the information, products, services, or related graphics contained in this Book for any purpose. Any use of this information is at your own risk.

The methods describe within this Book are the author's personal thoughts. They are not intended to be a definitive set of instructions for this project. You may discover there are other methods and materials to accomplish the same end result.

The author has made every effort to ensure the accuracy of the information within this book was correct at time of publication. The author and publisher do not assume and hereby disclaims any liability to any party for any loss, damage, or disruption caused by errors or omissions, whether such errors or omissions result from accident, negligence, or any other cause.

Sun Media Group, LLC
First Book Publication Date: 6/2020
Cover Illustration: T. Irvolino
To contact Author, please email publisher: sunmediagroupllc@gmail.com

Henna Tattoo Stencil Transfer

Items needed:
- A blank sheet of paper
- A ballpoint pen
  Make sure it's ballpoint; other pens won't work
- A clear deodorant stick - no sprays
- Printed design from this book
- Scissors

Directions

1. Place the white piece of paper over the printed design and trace over the entire design.

2. Cut out your design with scissors.

3. Apply a thin layer of clear deodorant on the area where you want the tattoo.

4. Place the design face down and hold it firmly for about 5 seconds.

5. Carefully remove the paper stencil.

6. Trace over the outline with your henna paste or jagua gel .

When tracing over the design with the henna paste, be careful not to touch it with your hand as it may rub off.

DESIGNS CAN ALSO BE CUT AND RAN THROUGH A THERMAL PRINTER AS WELL.

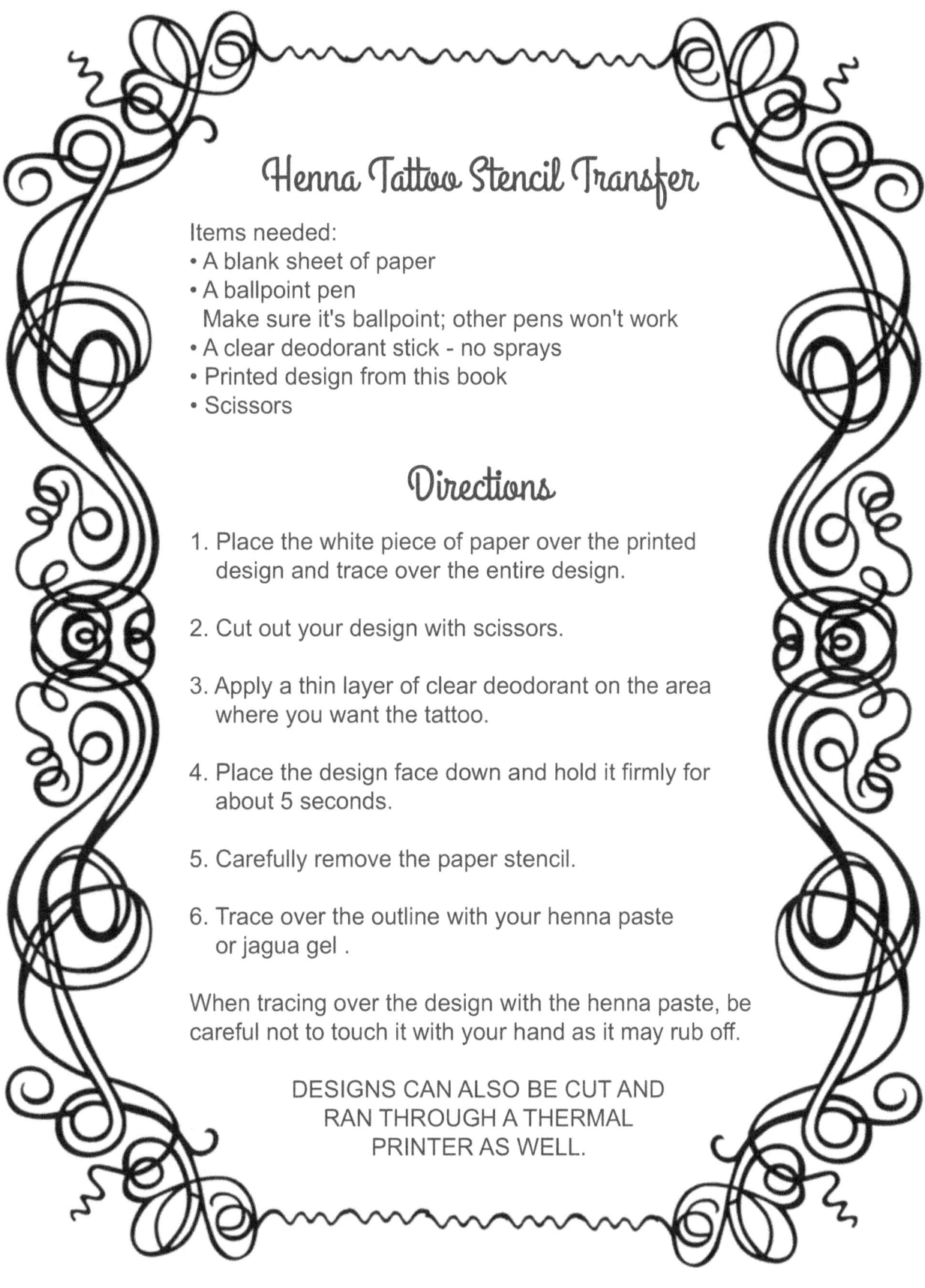

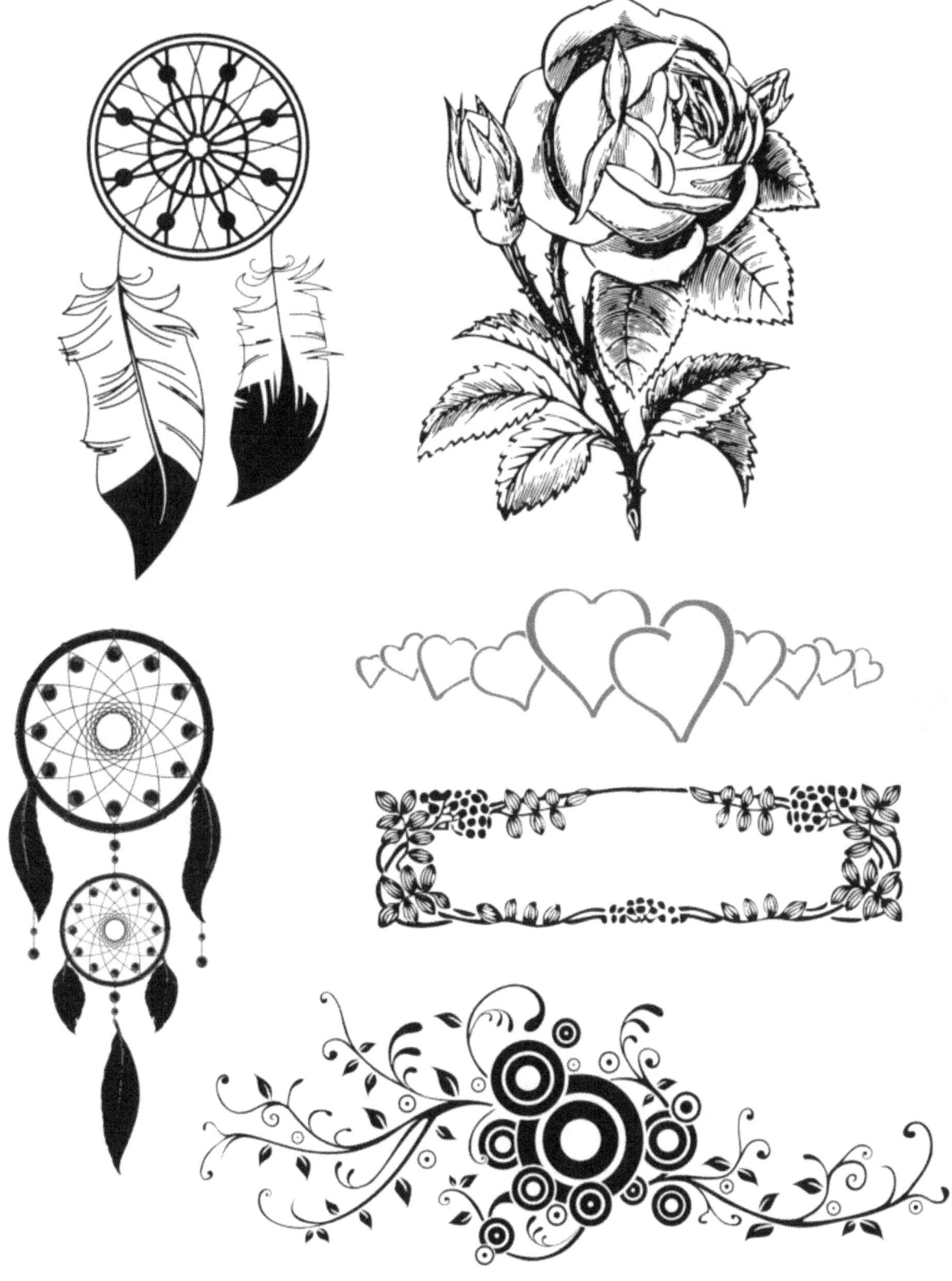

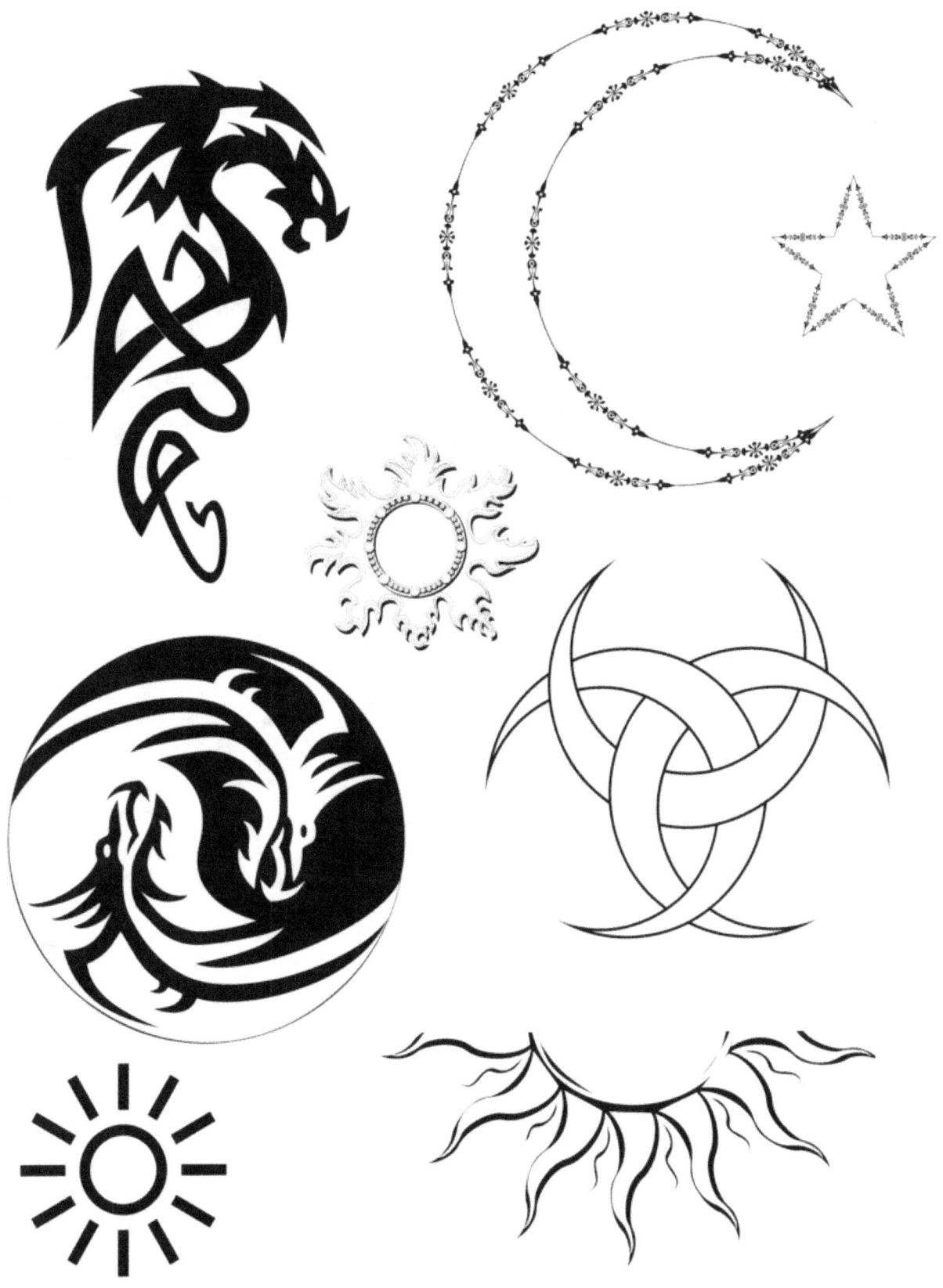

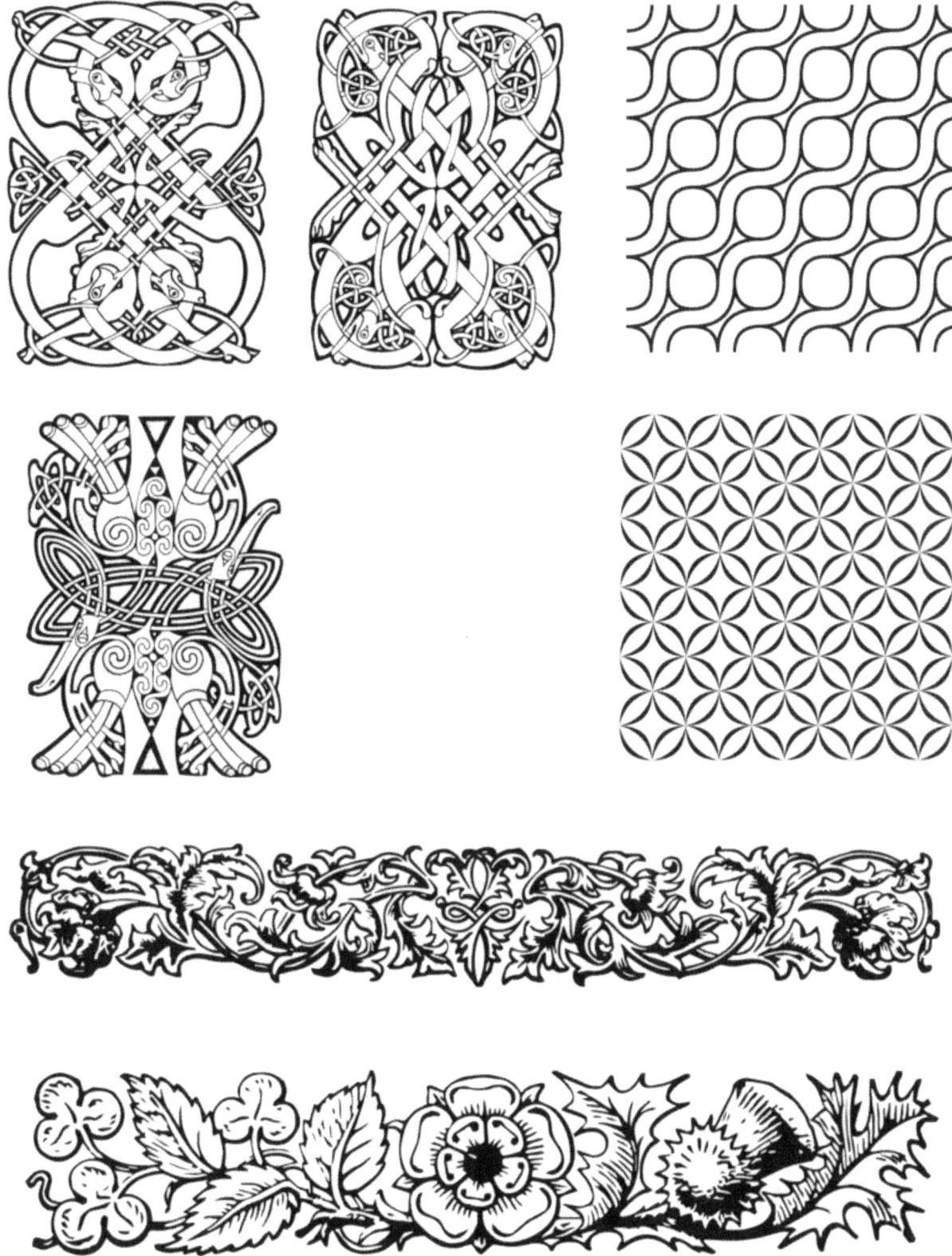

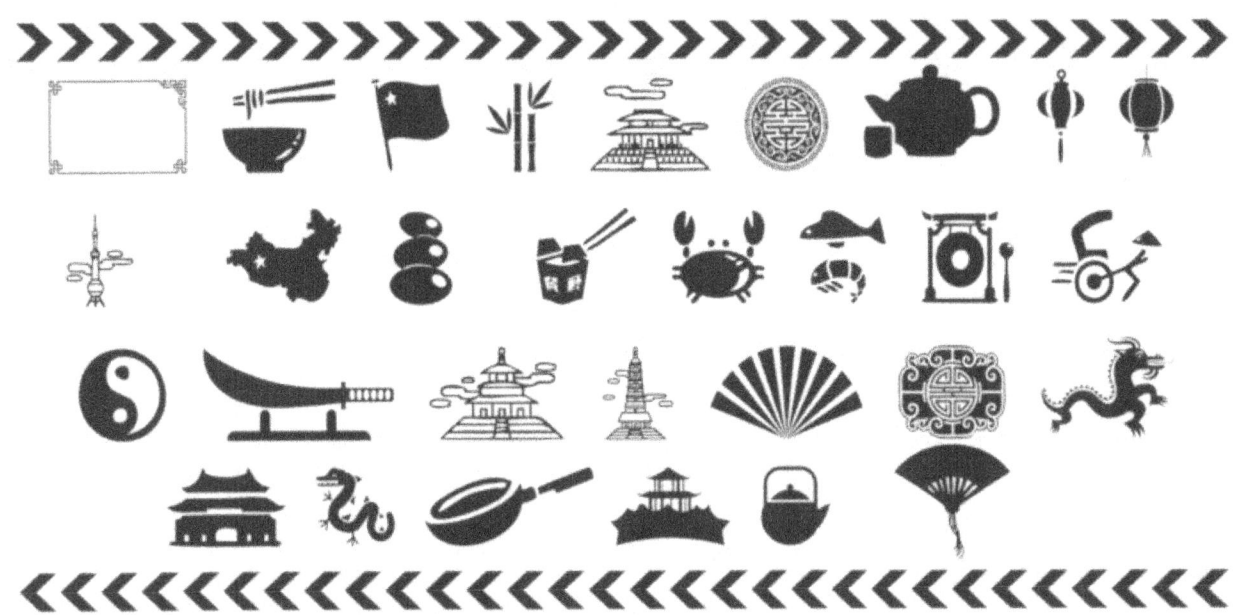
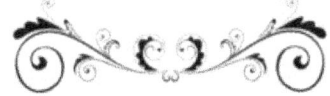

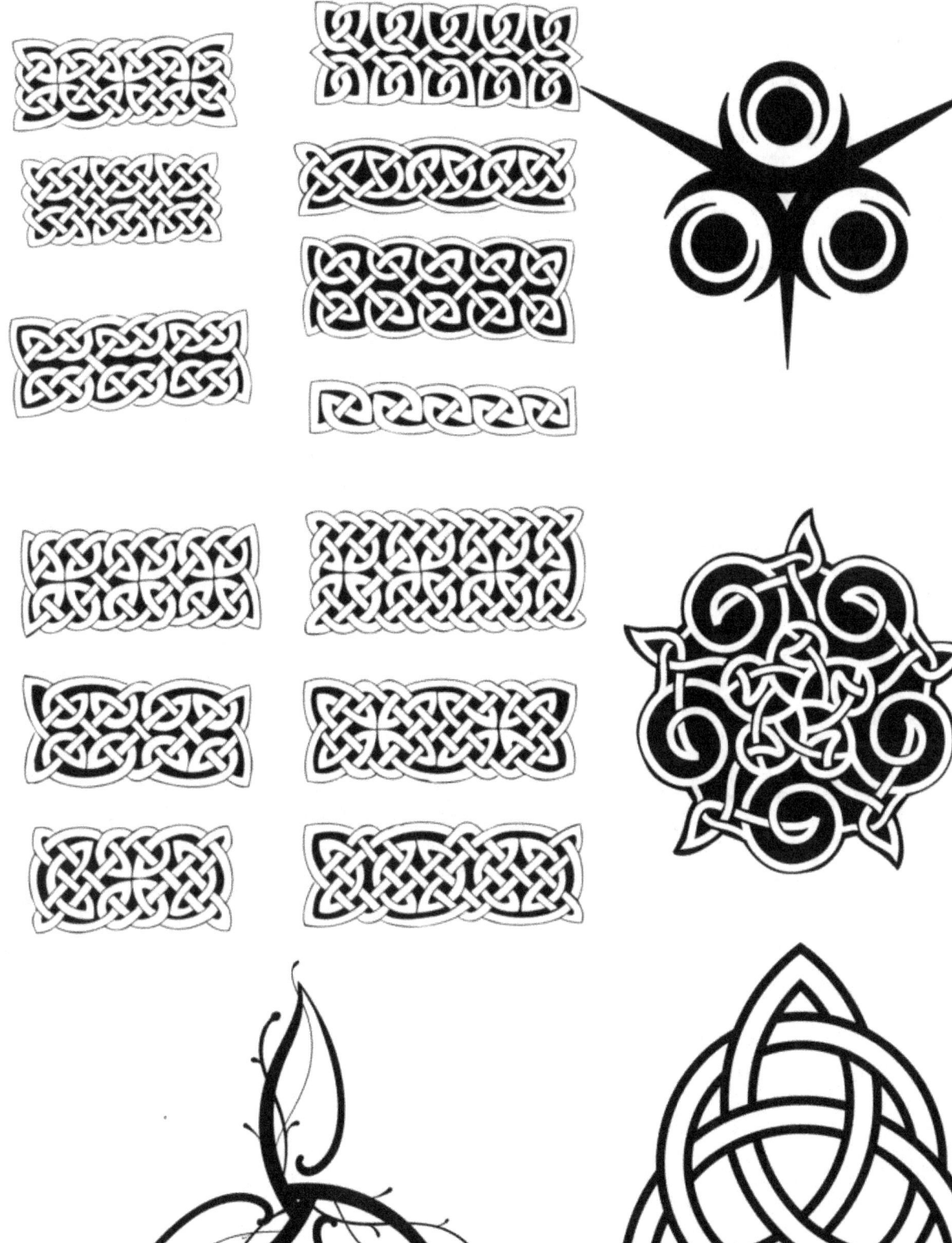

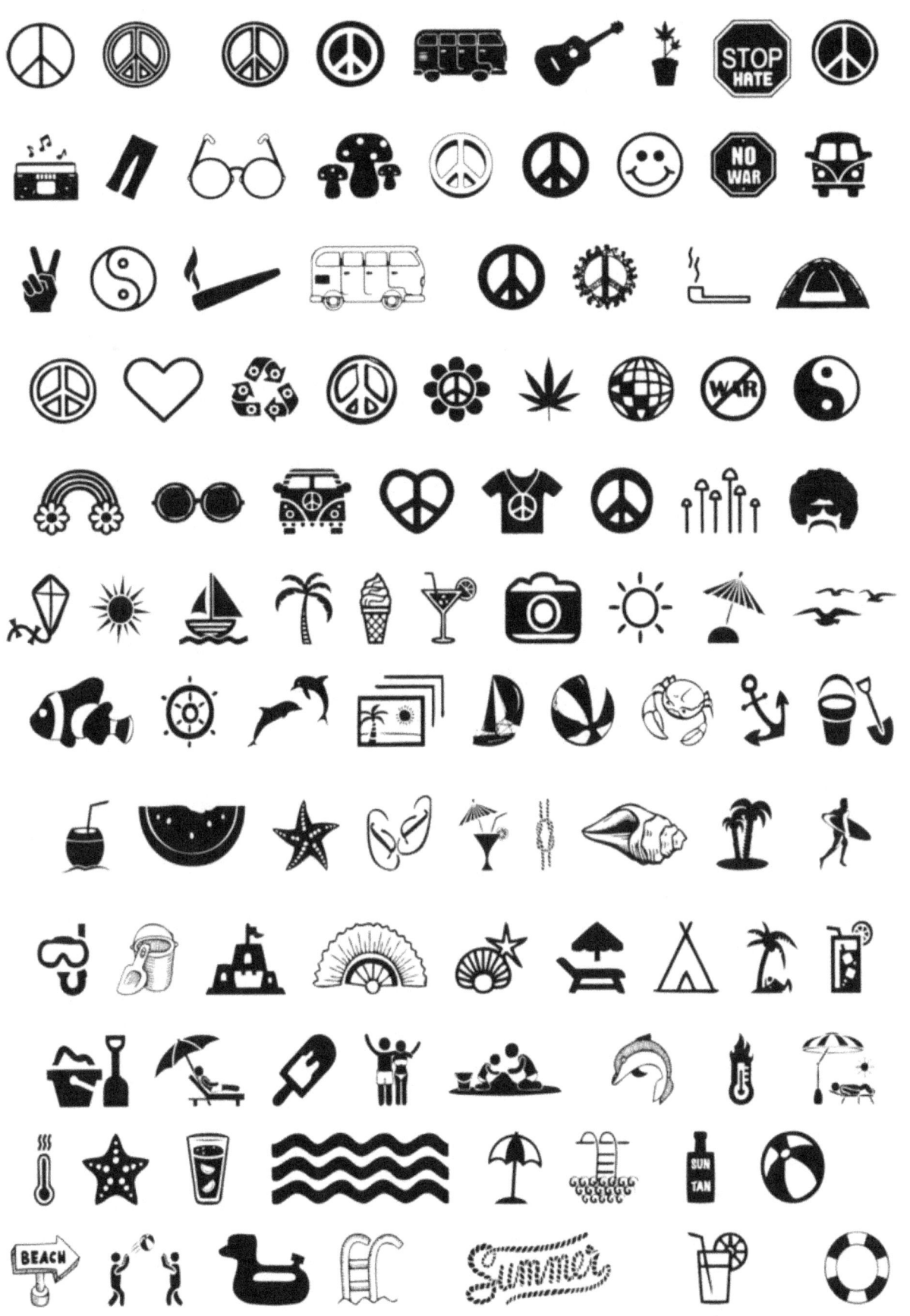

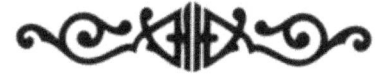

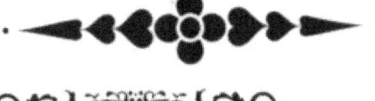

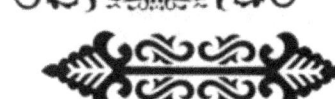
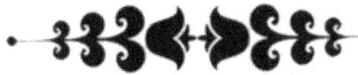

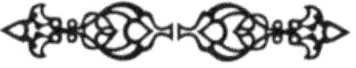

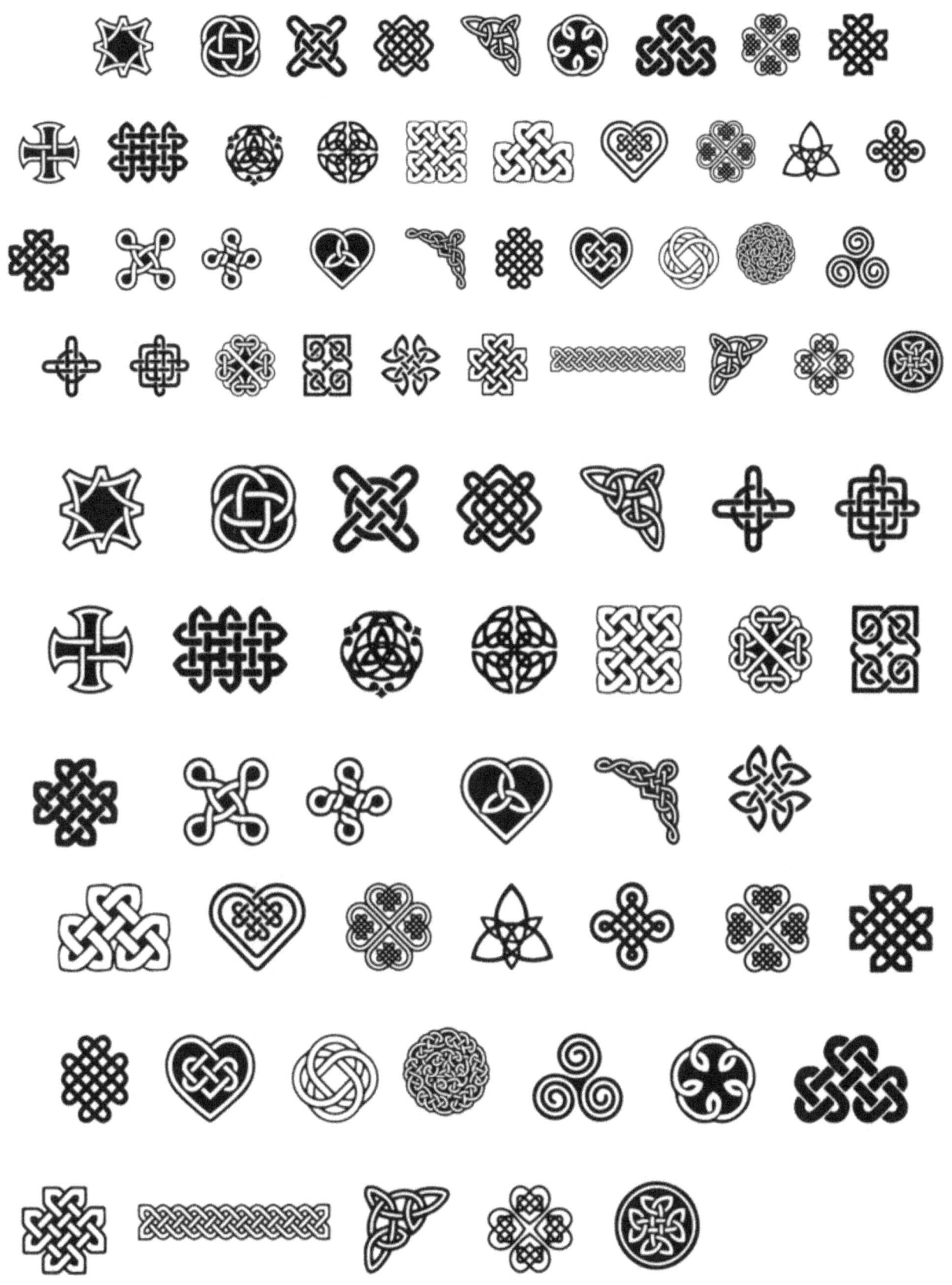

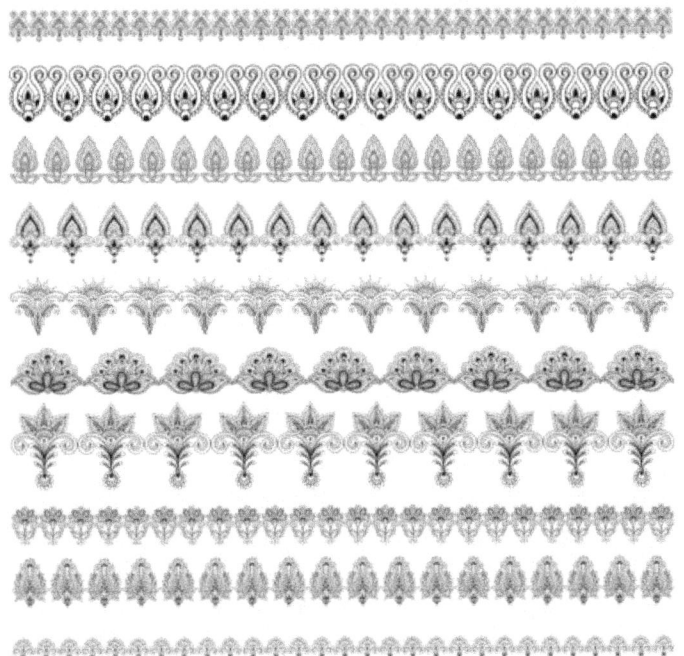

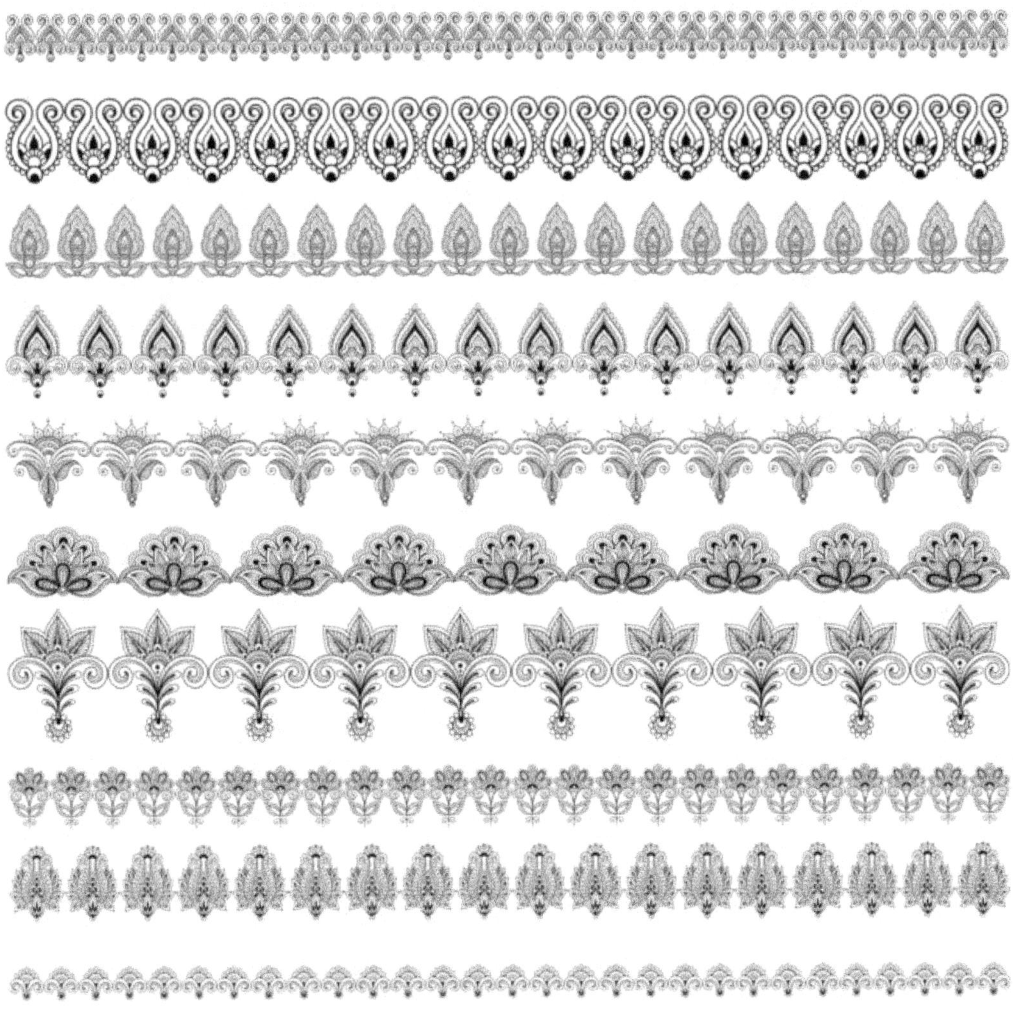

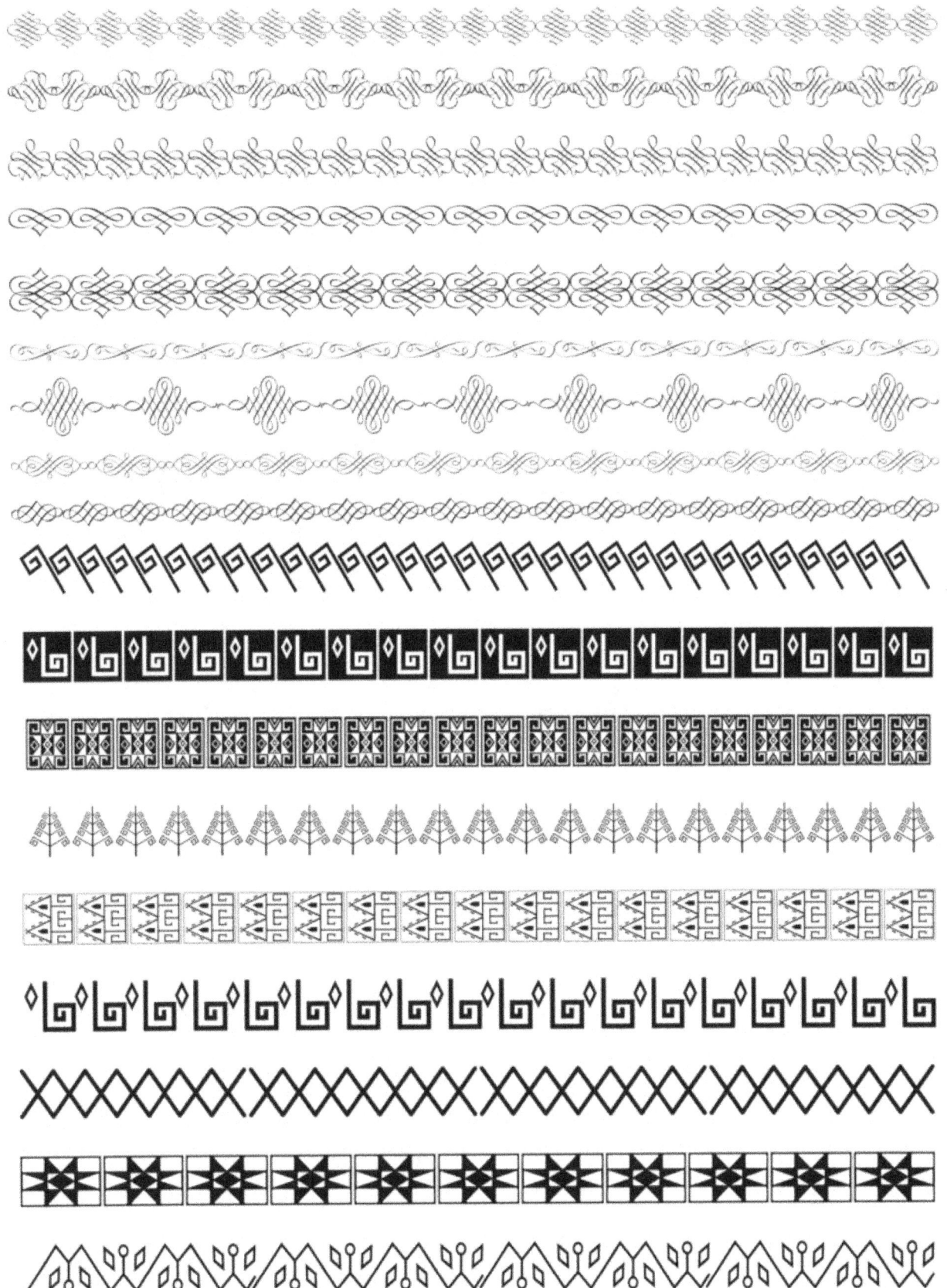

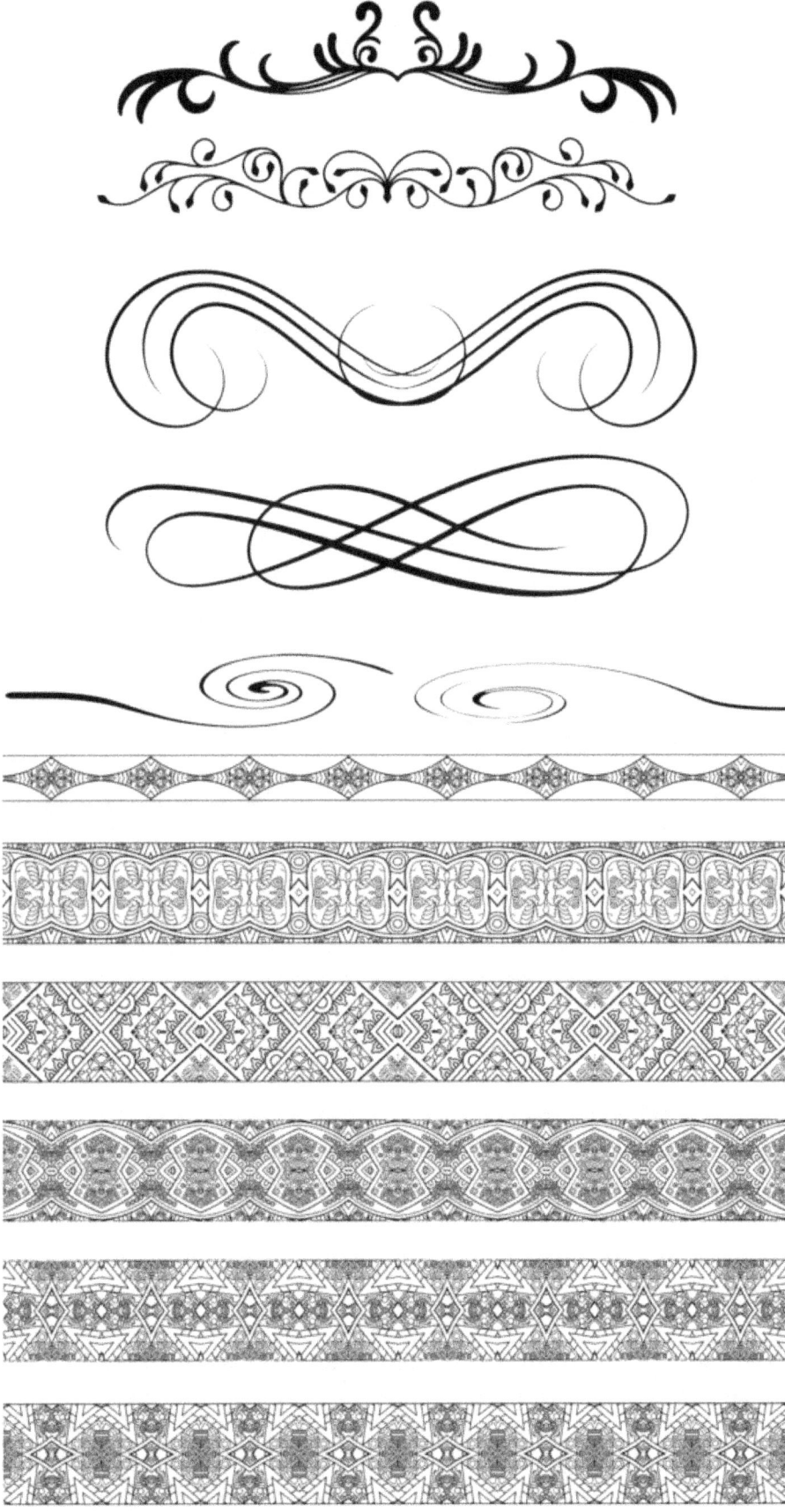

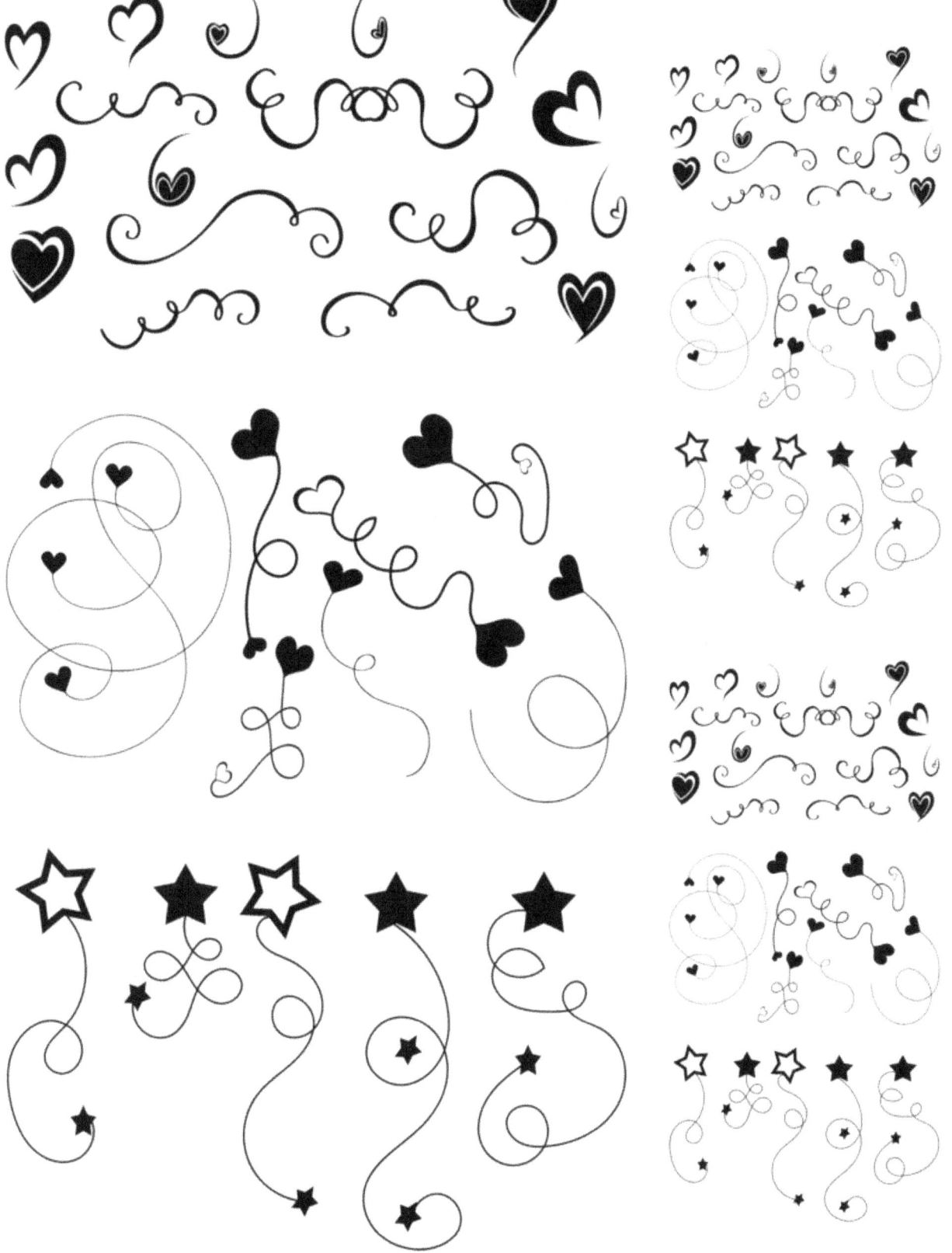

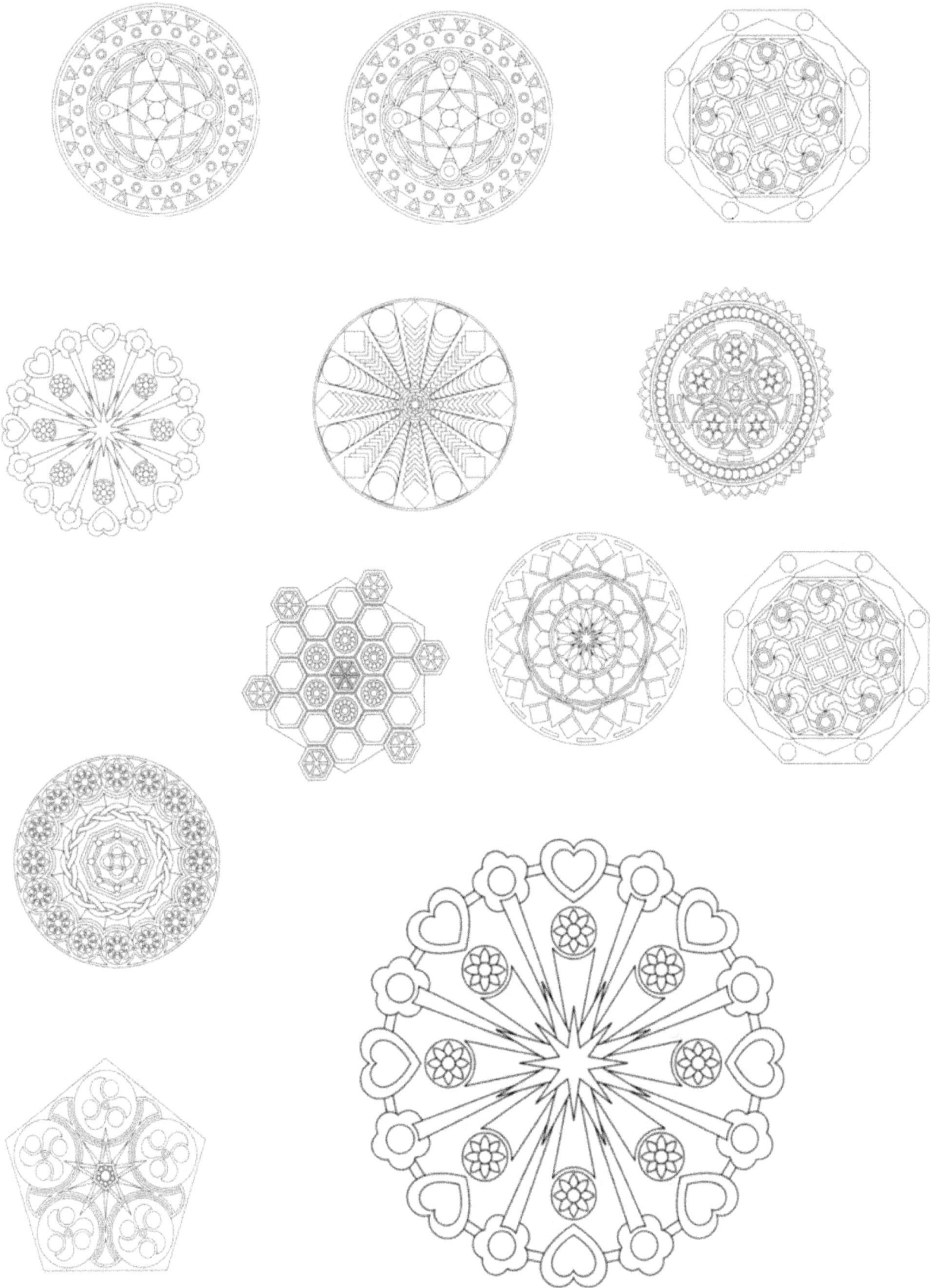

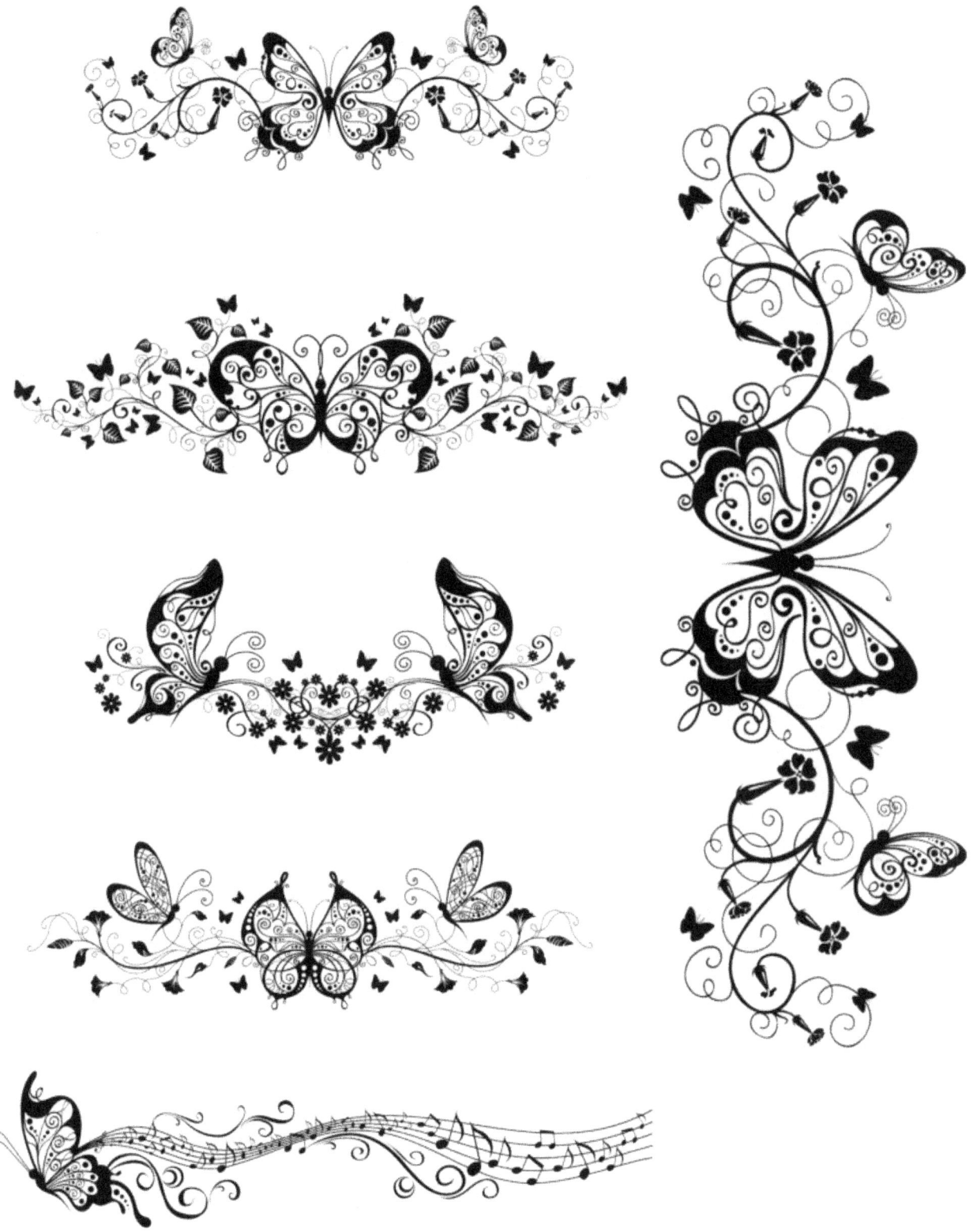

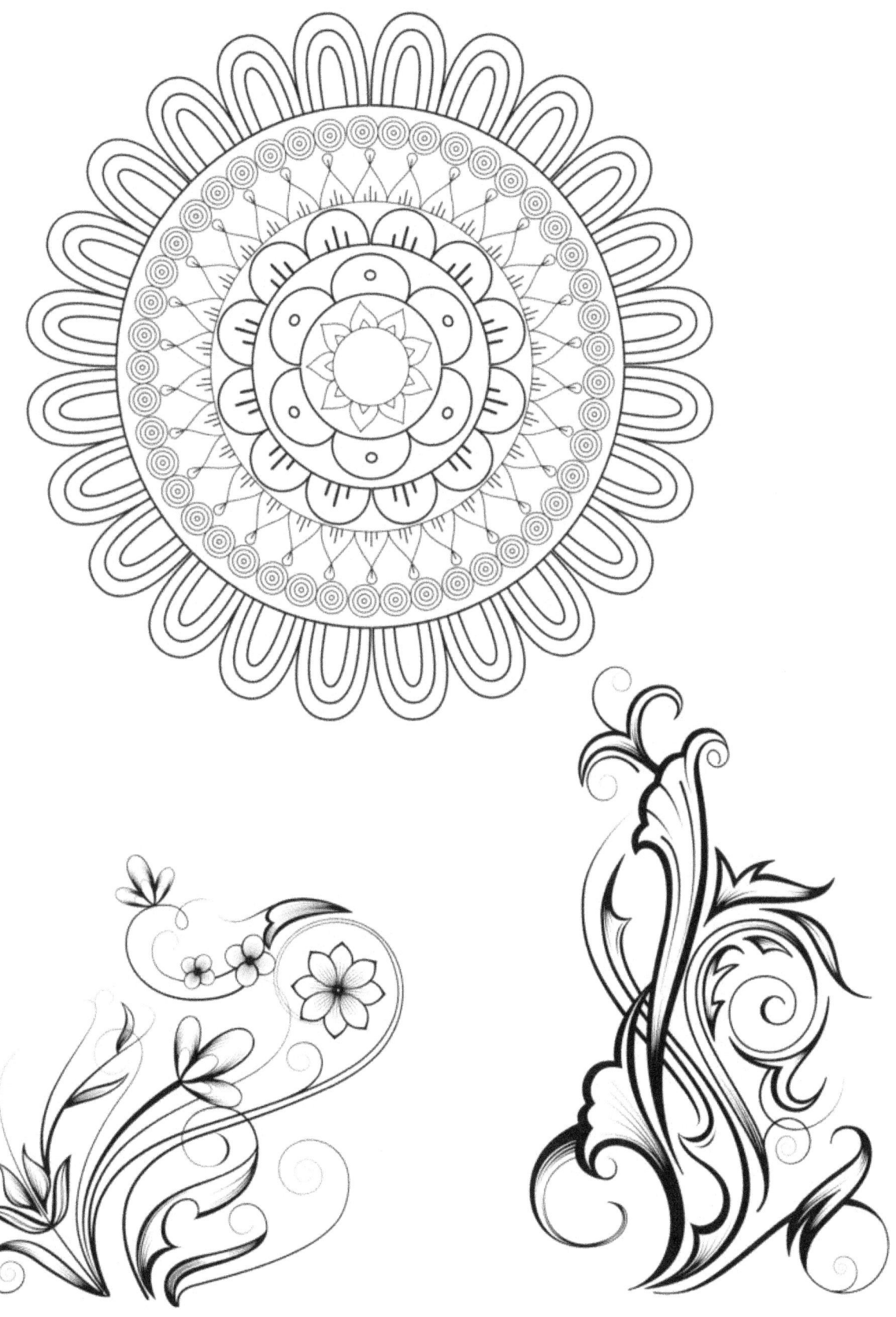

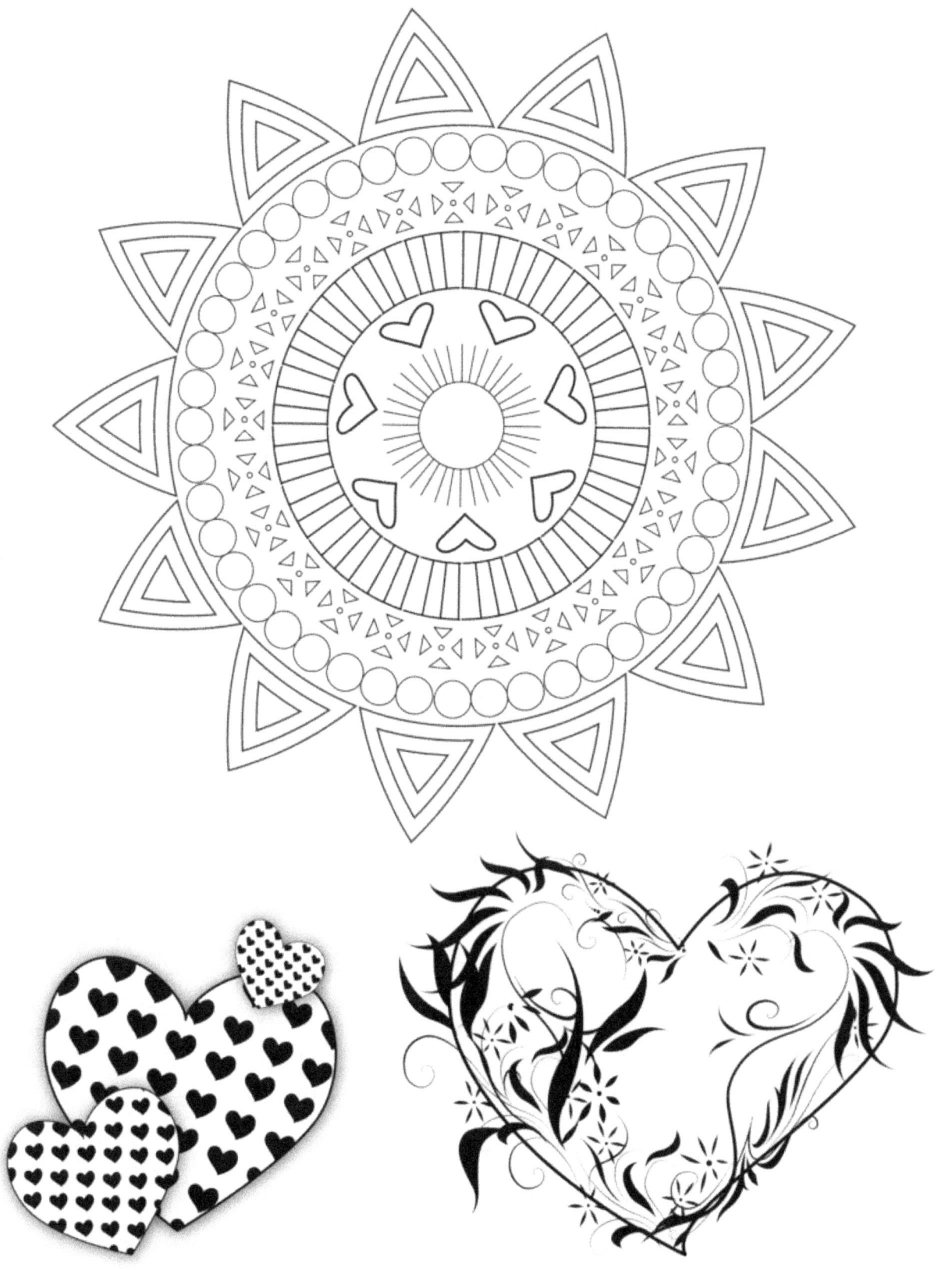

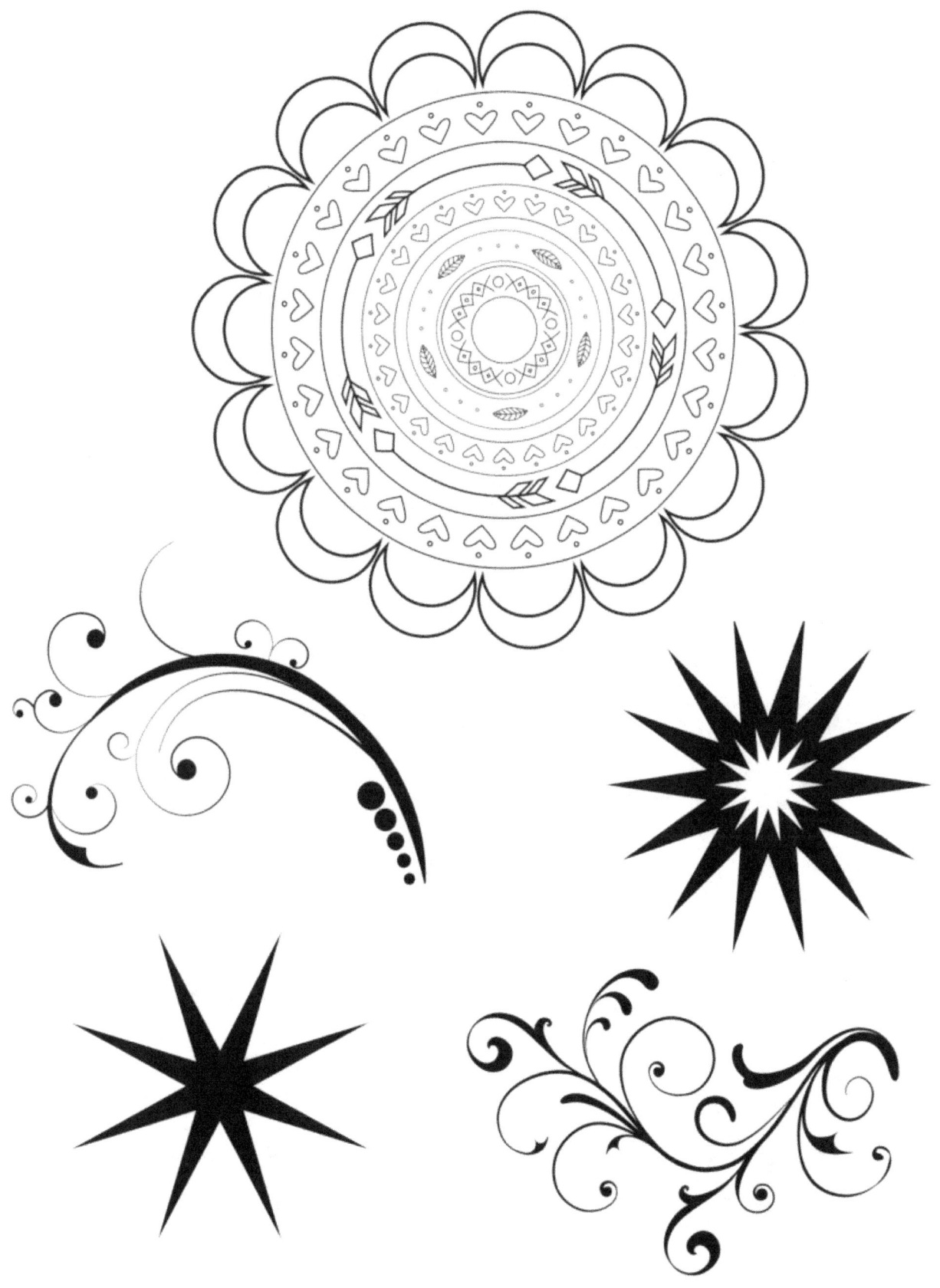

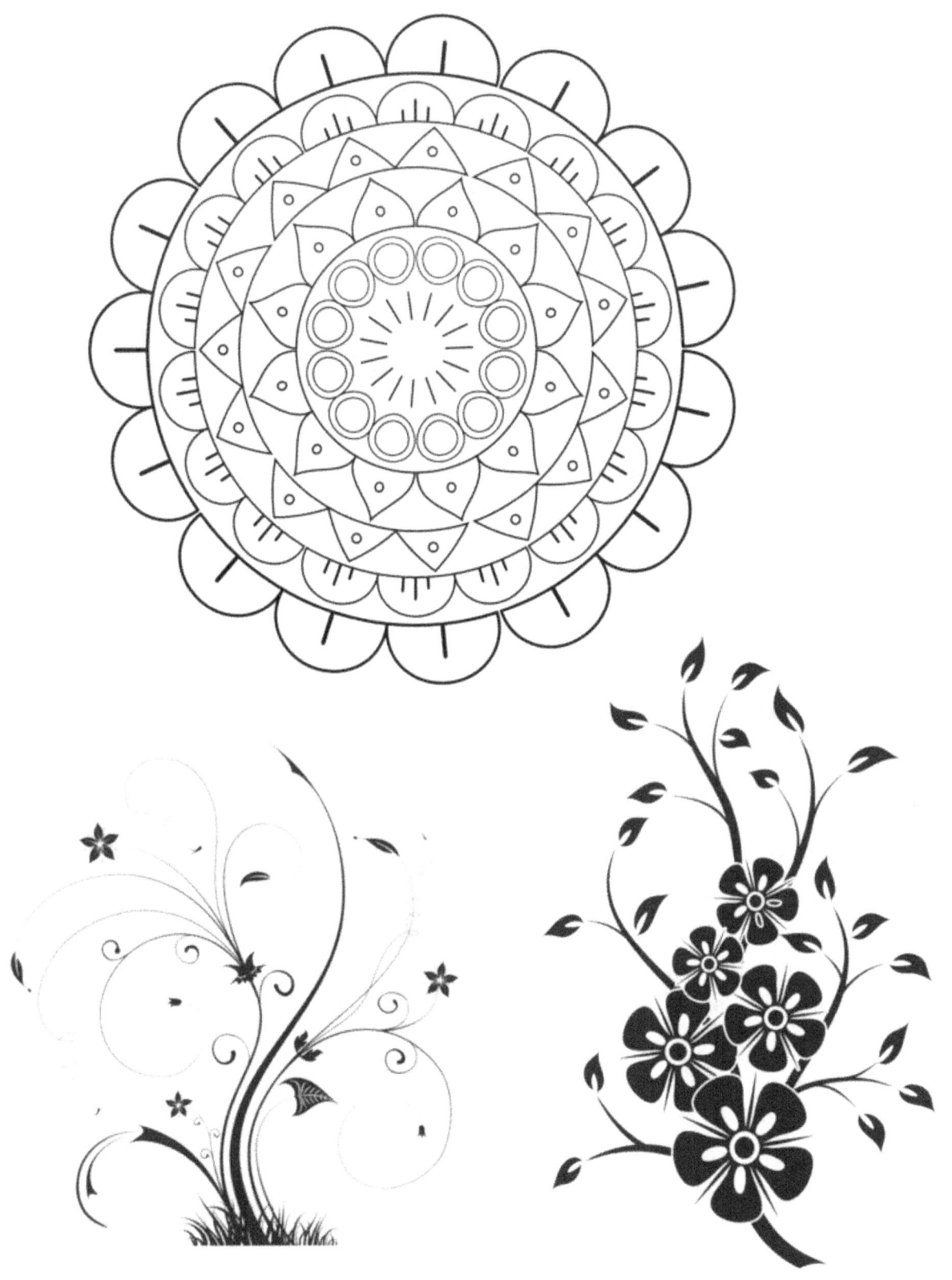

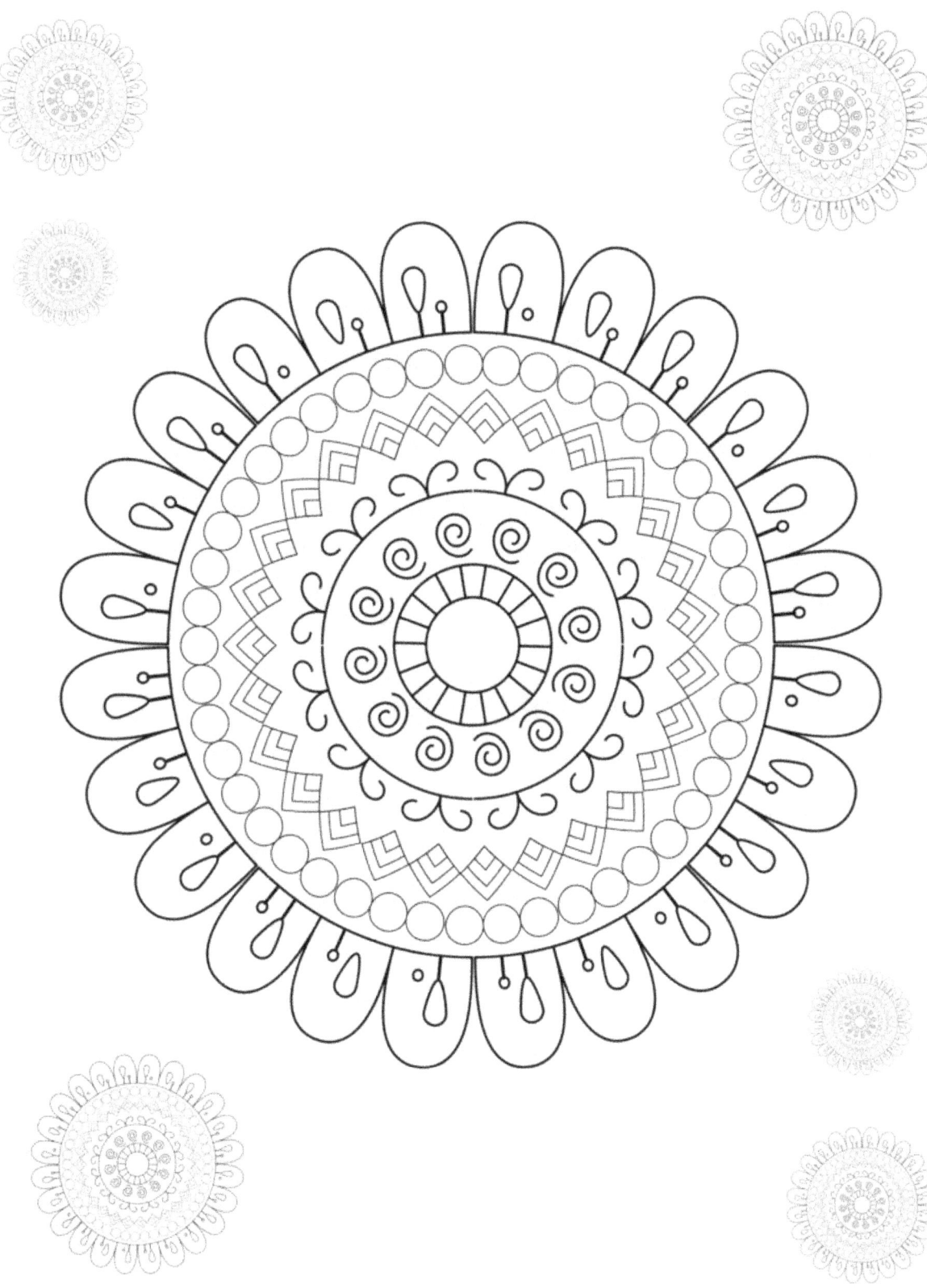

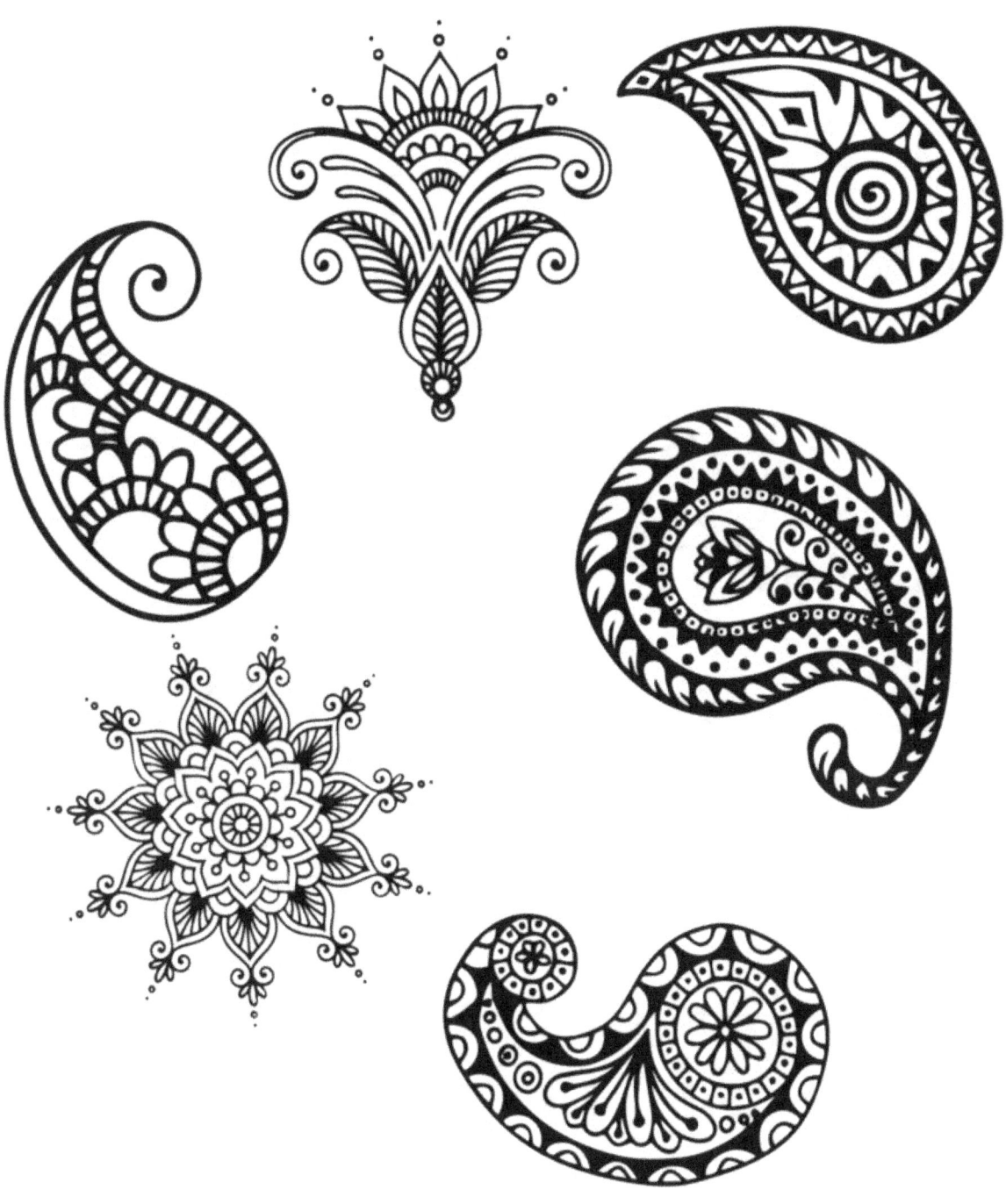

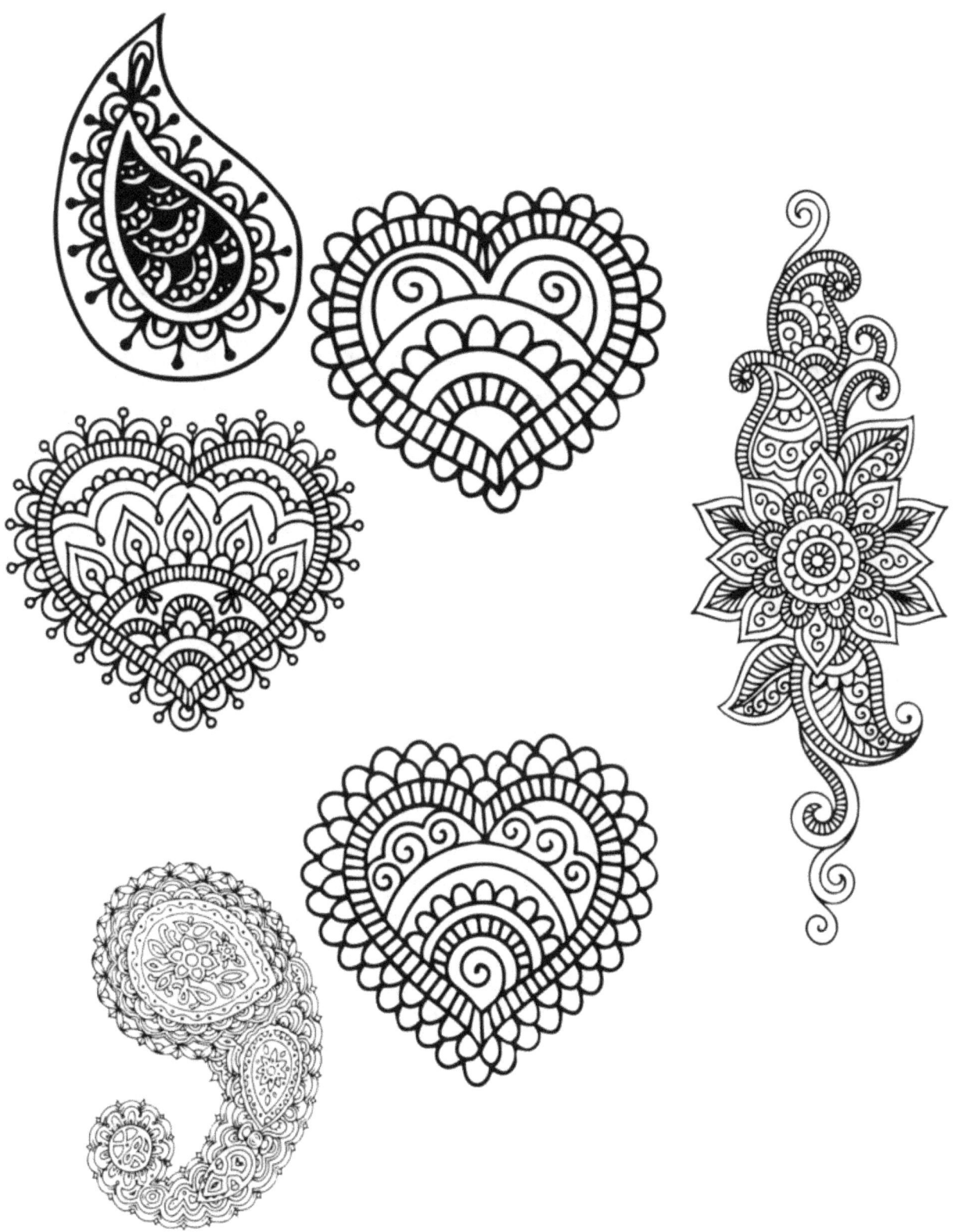

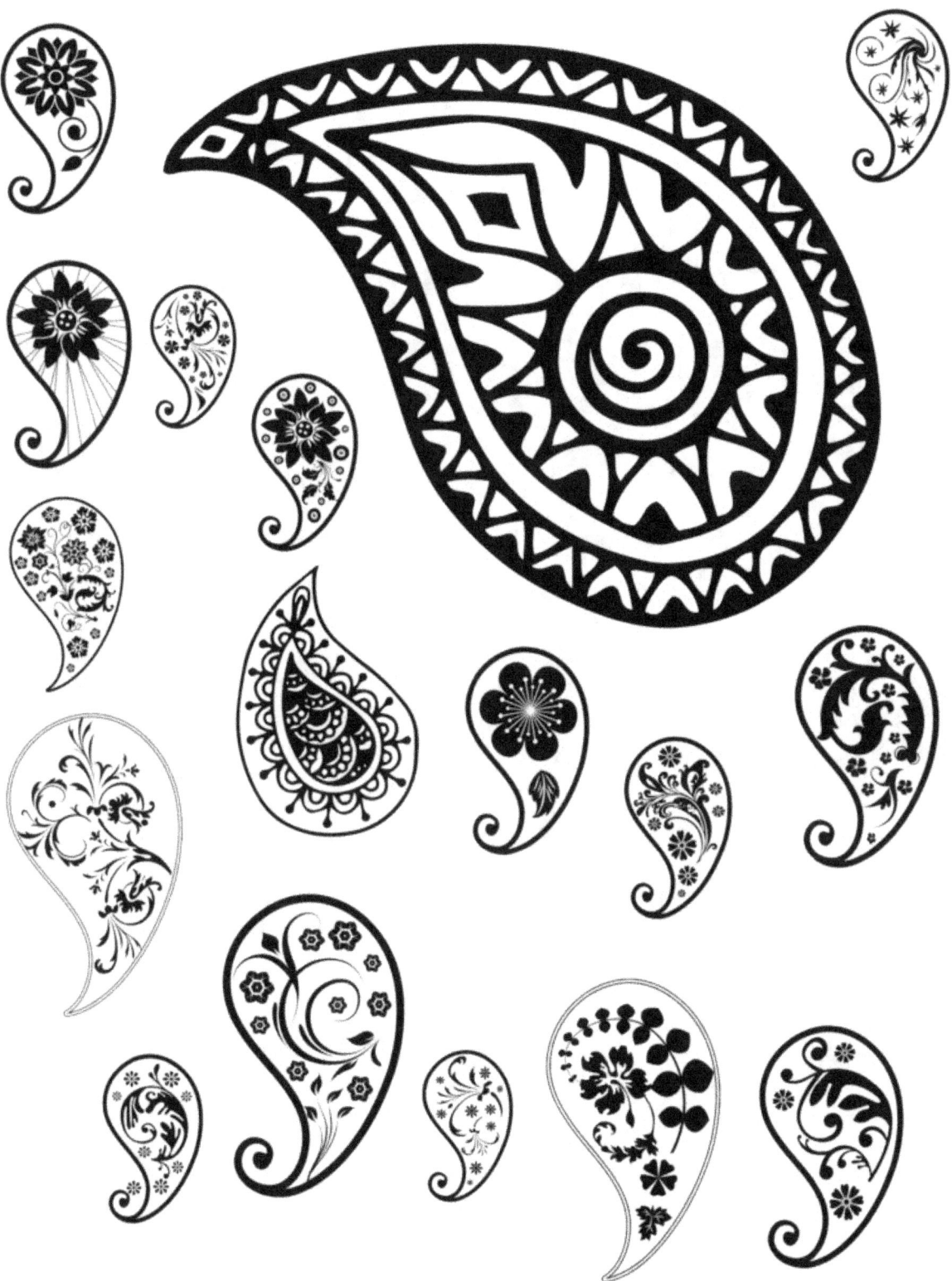

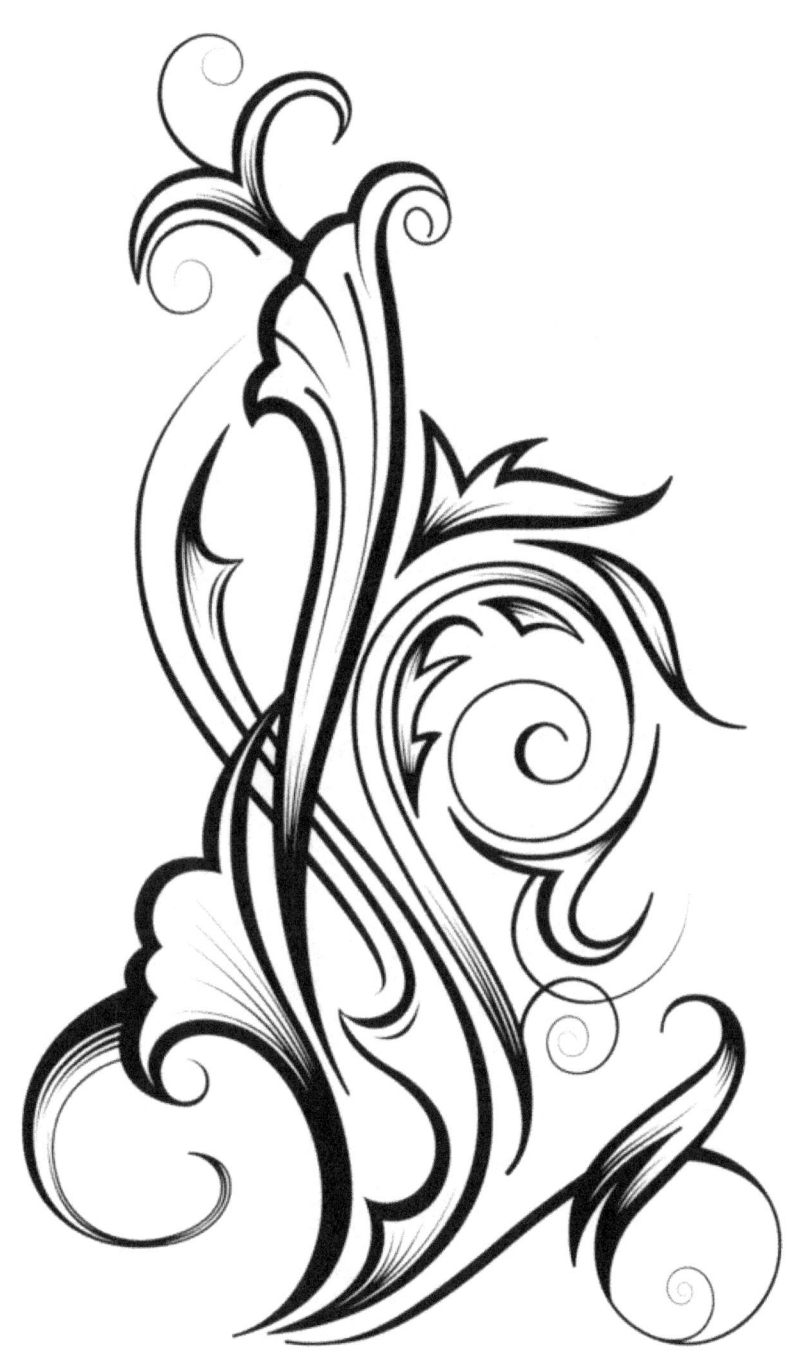

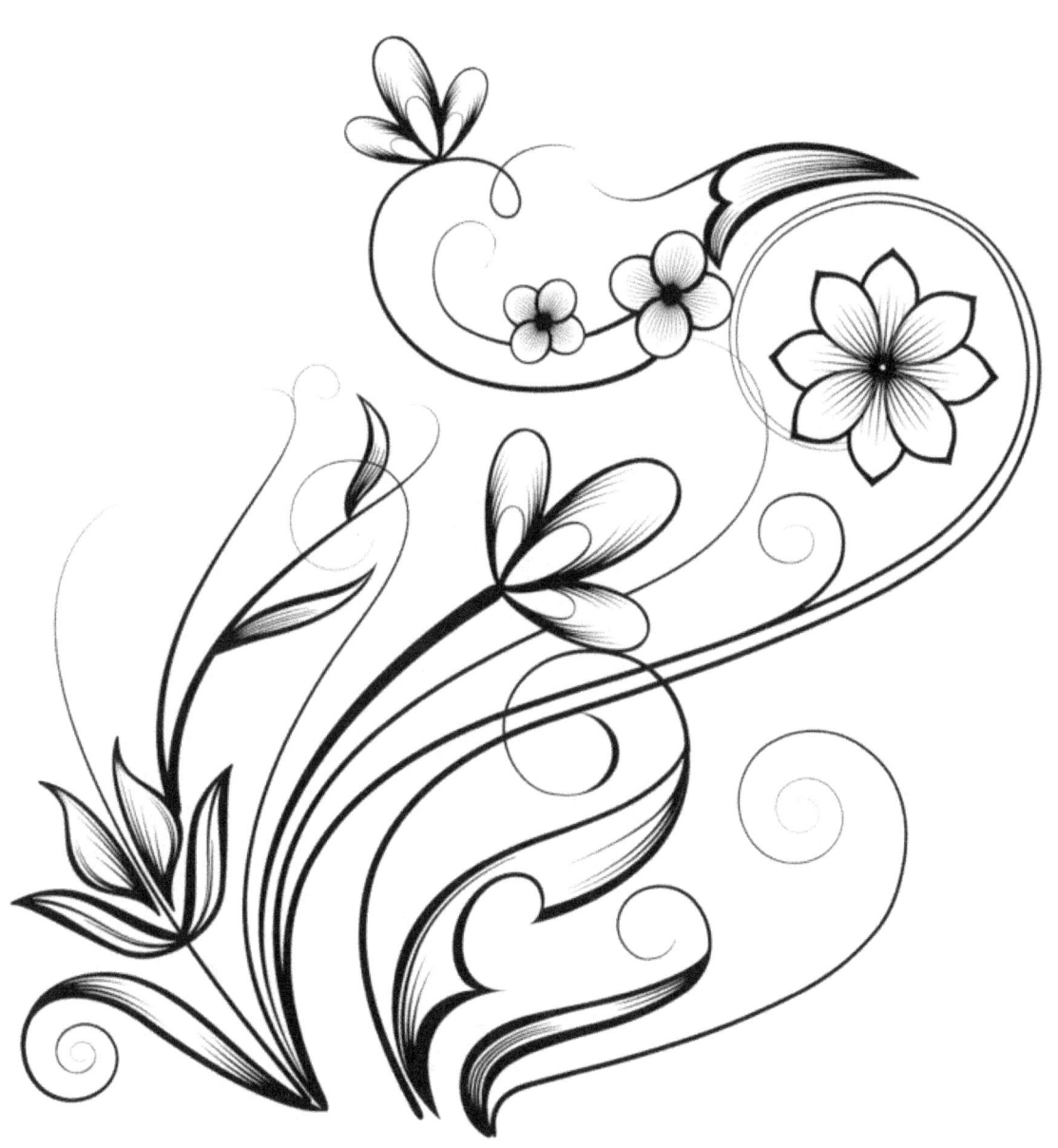

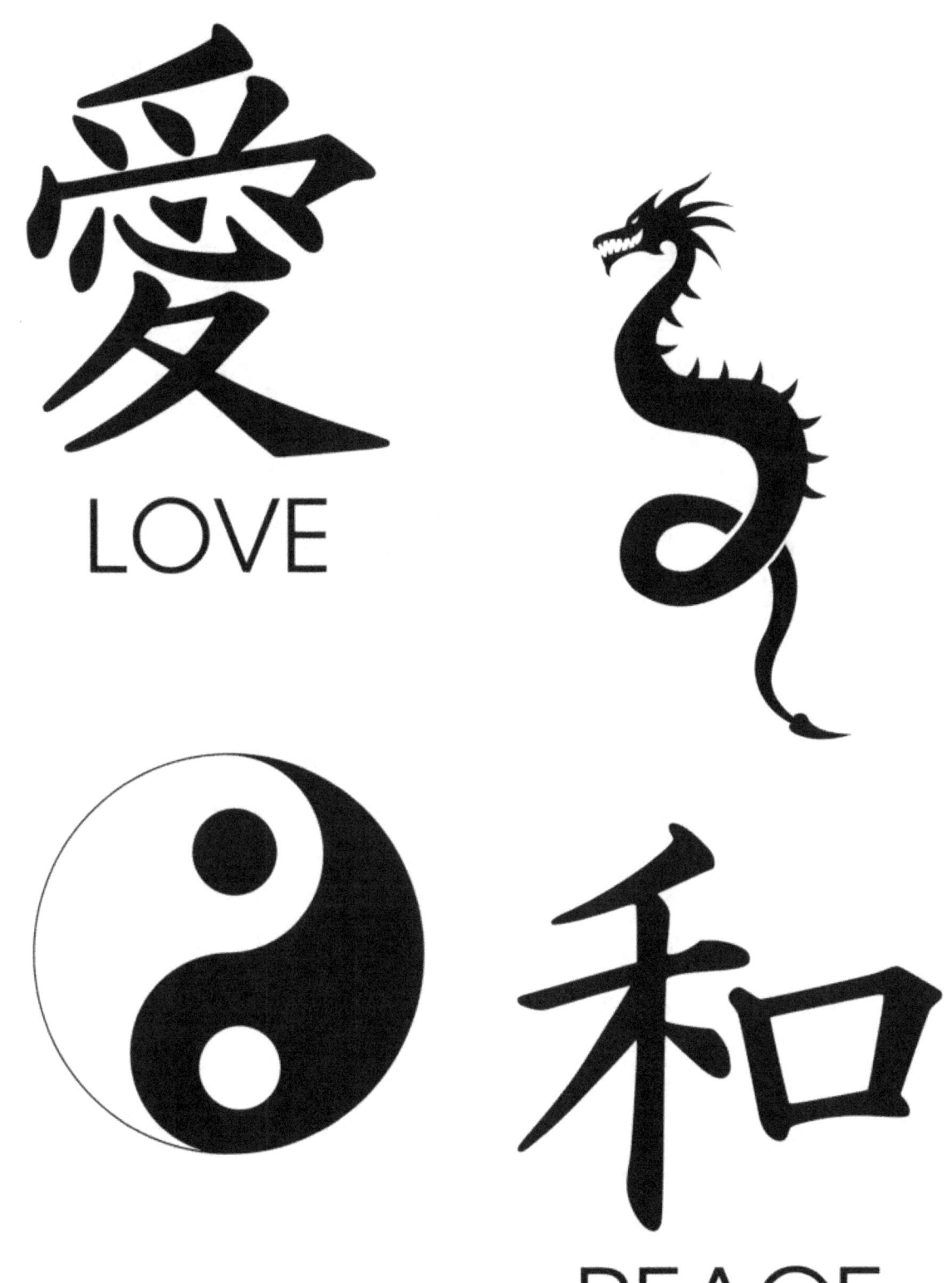

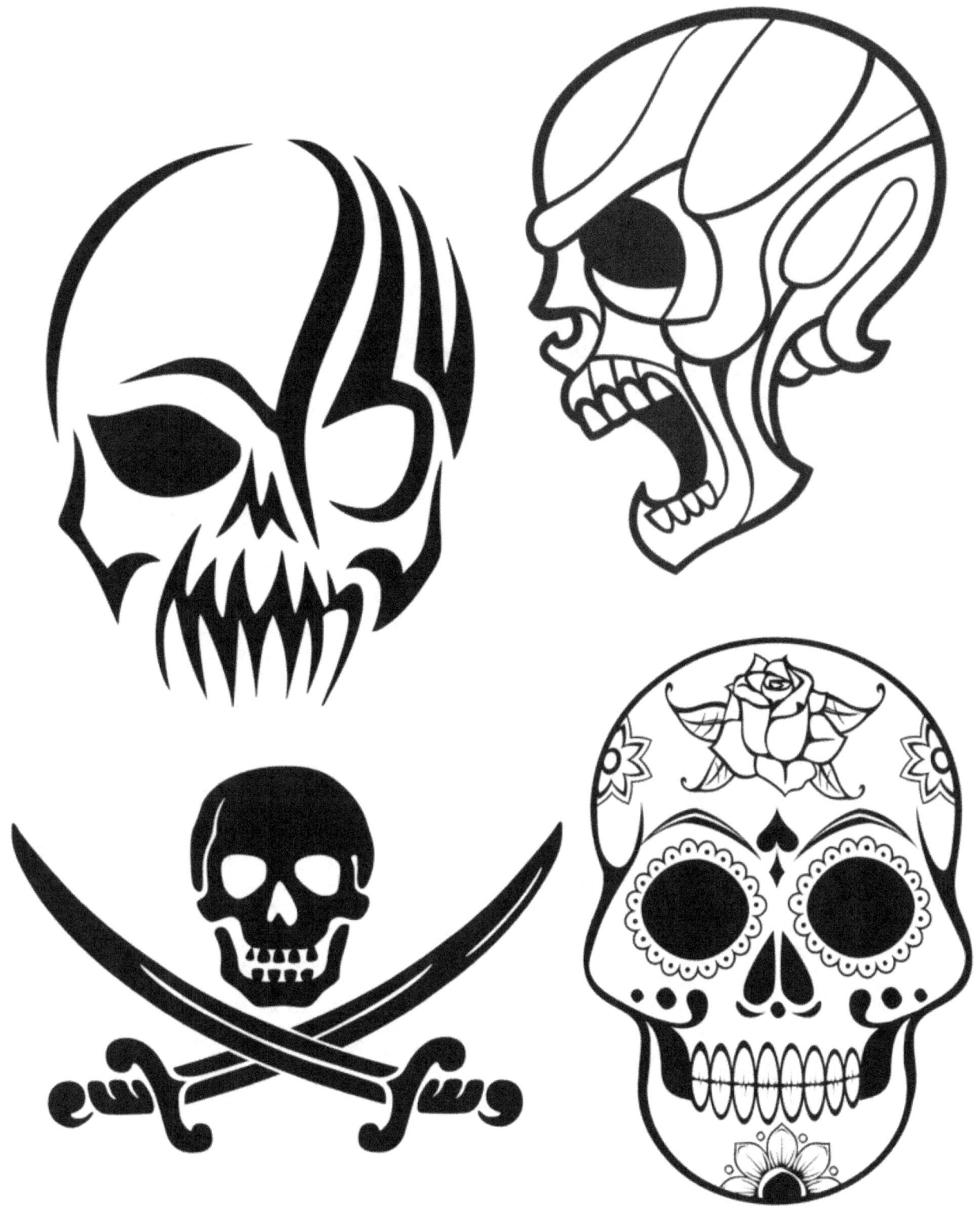

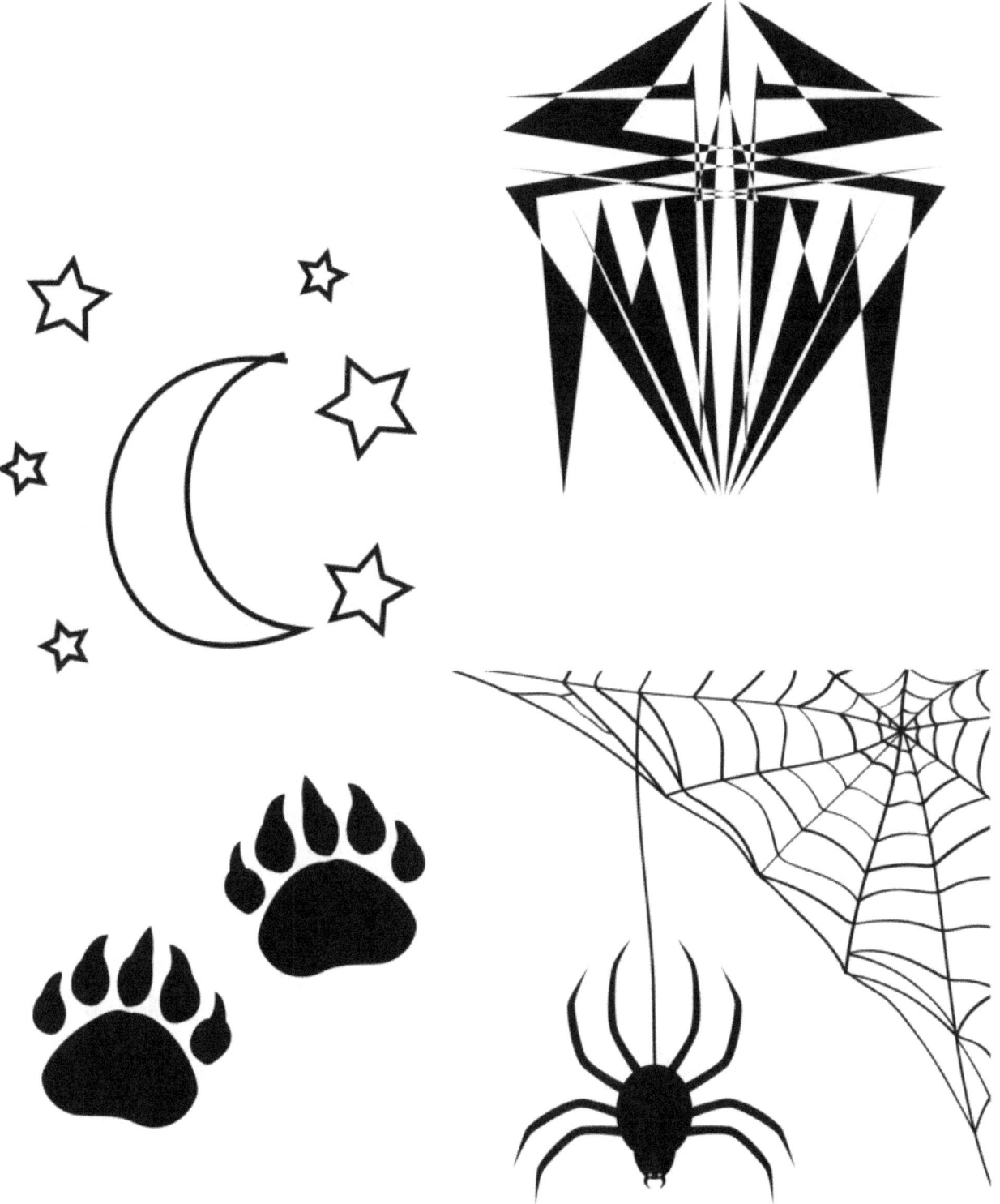

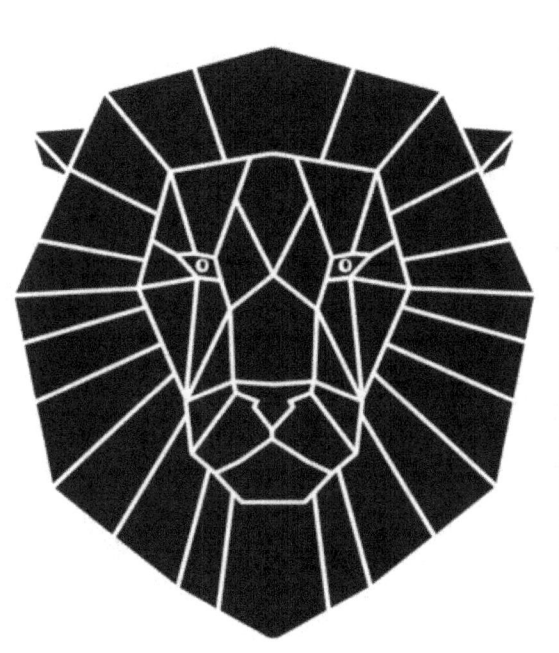
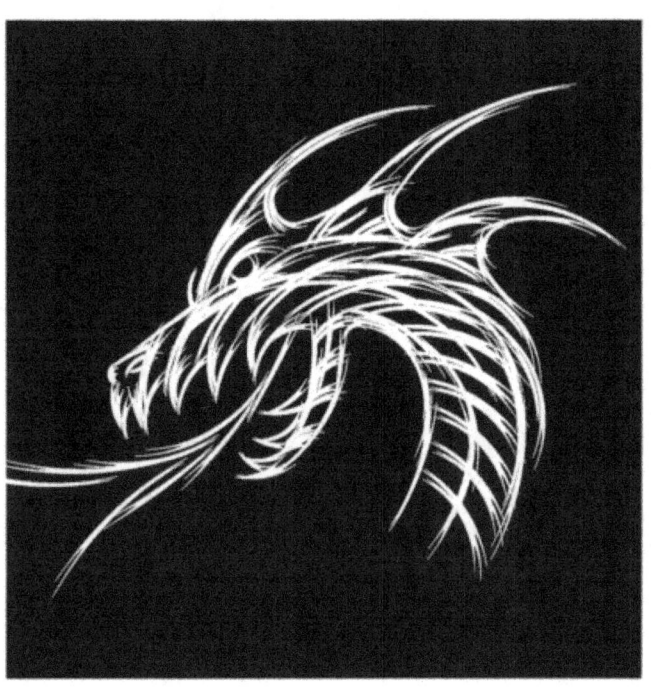
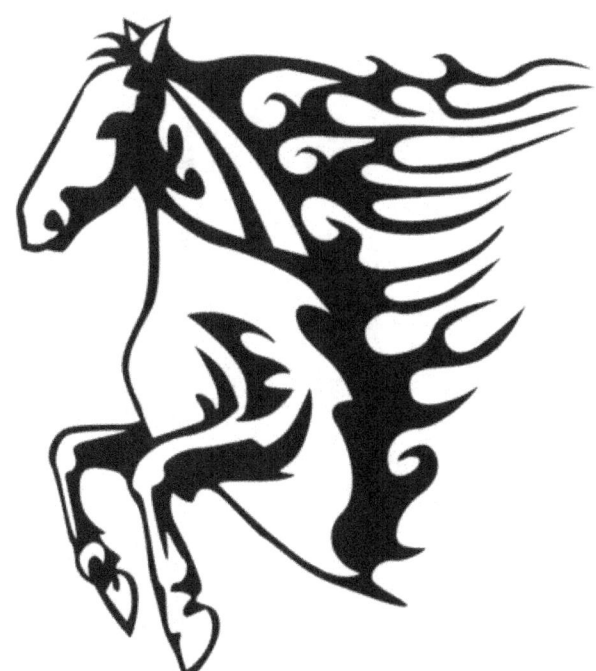
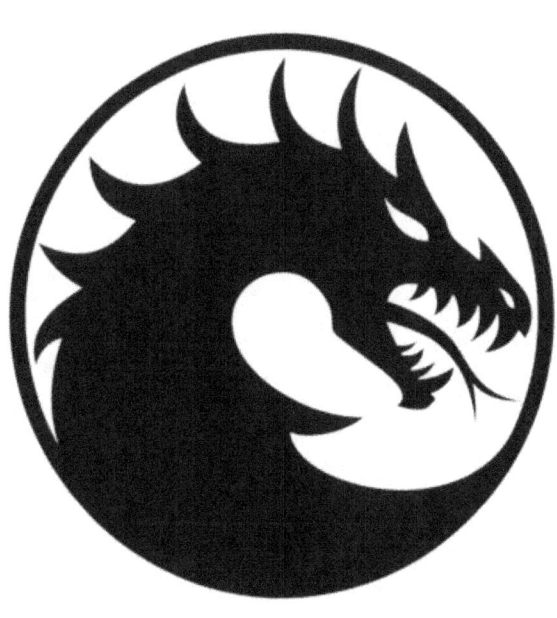

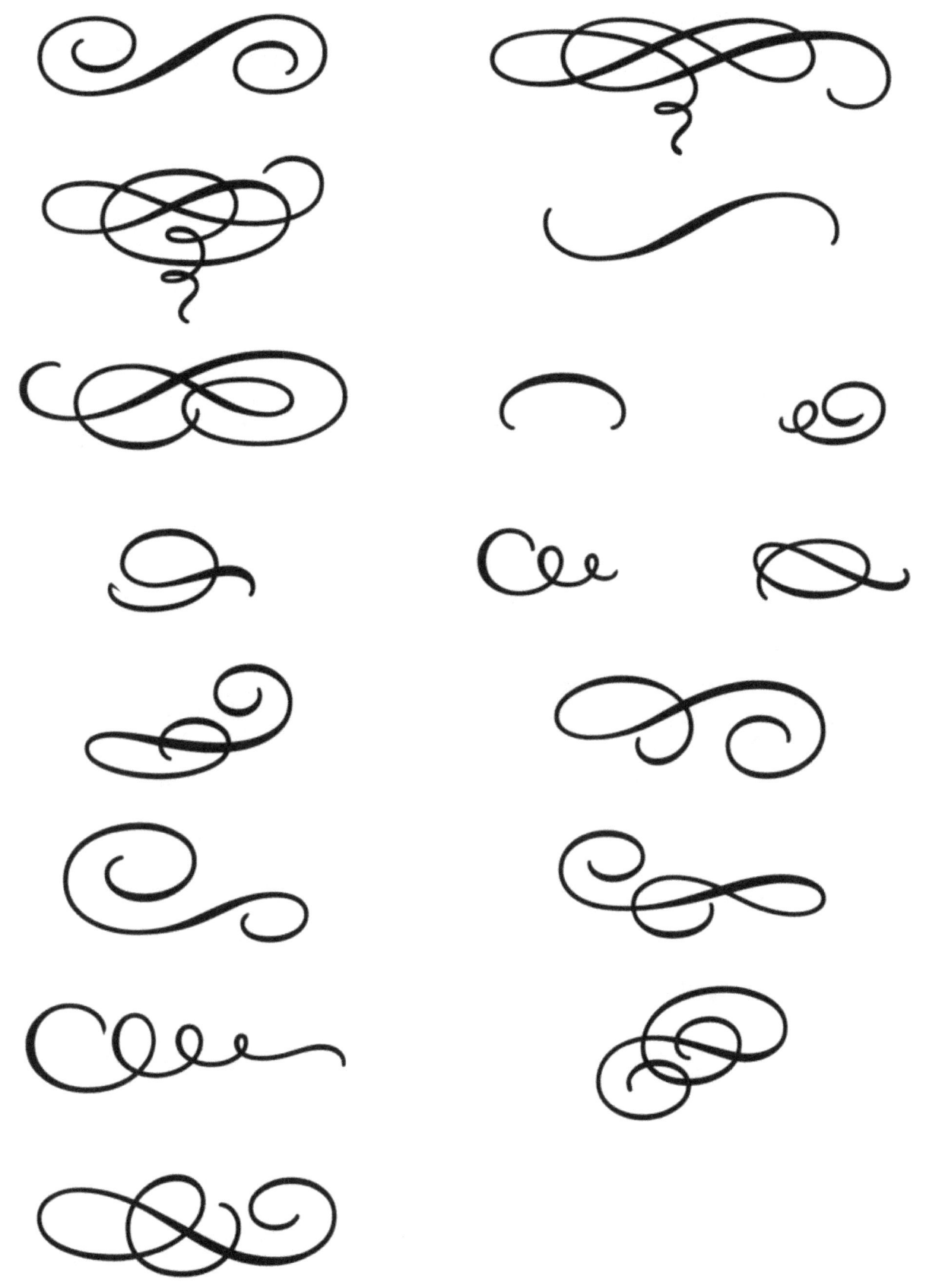

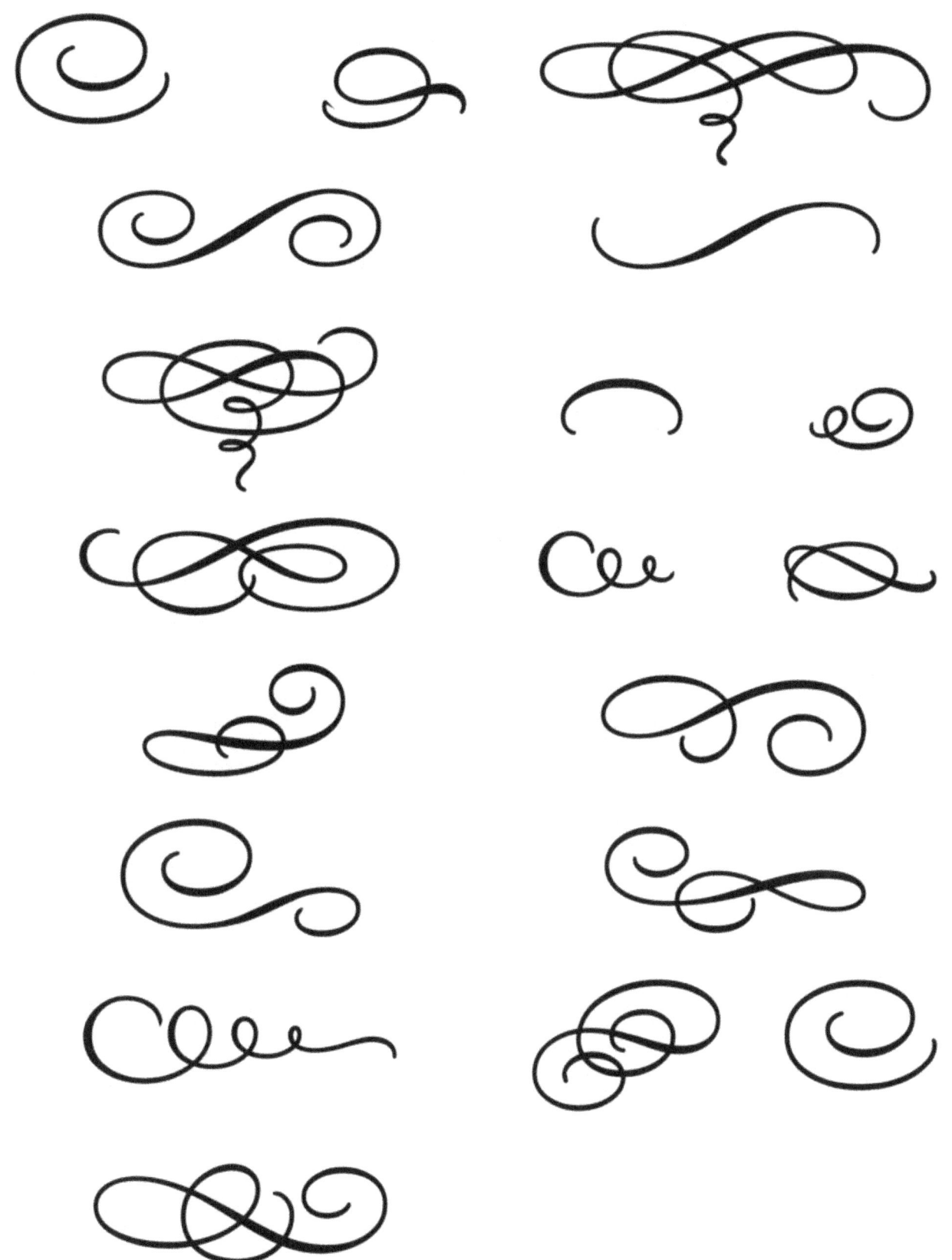

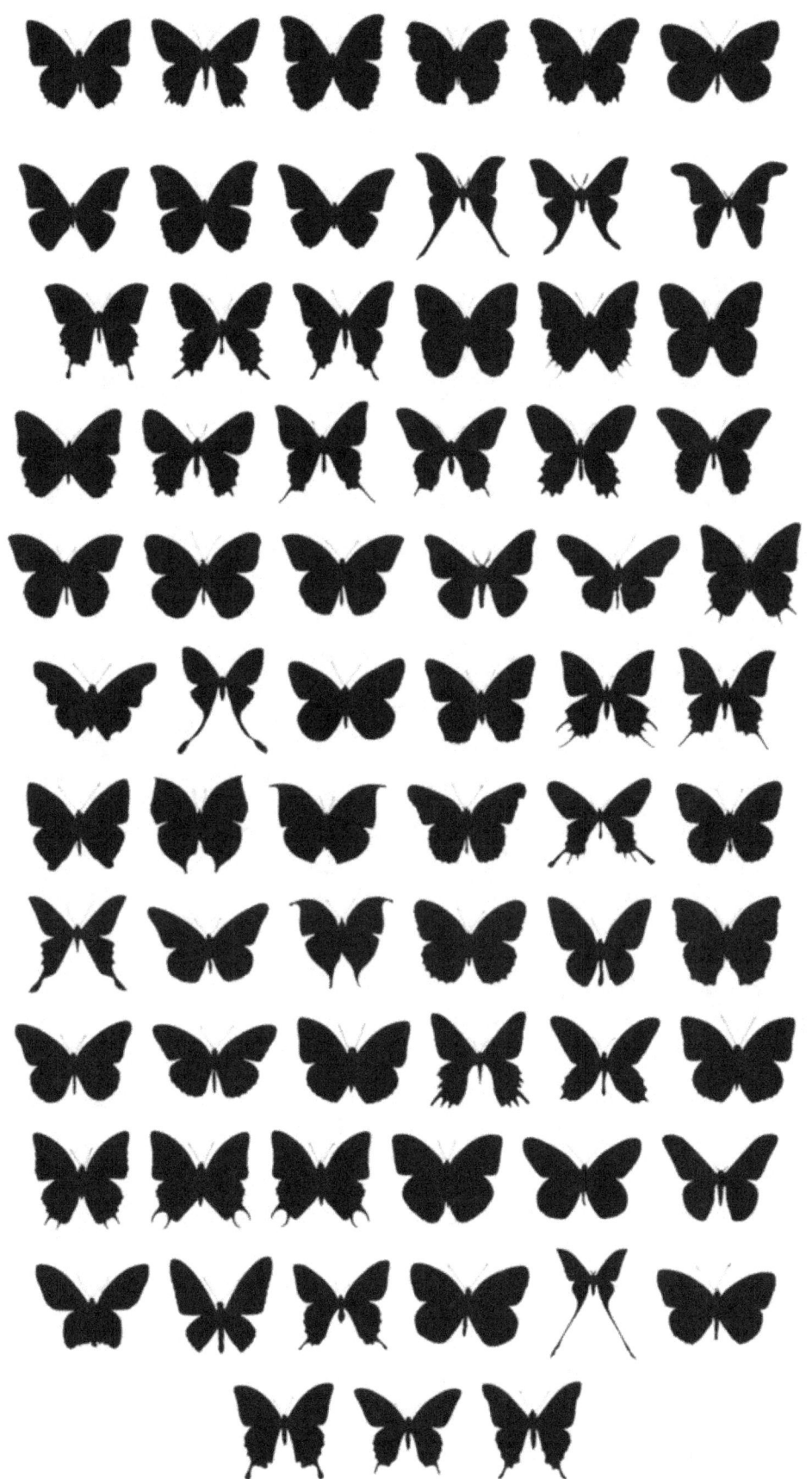

♈ ♉ ♊ ♋
♌ ♍ ♎ ♏
♐ ♑ ♒ ♓

♈ ♉ ♊ ♋
♌ ♍ ♎ ♏
♐ ♑ ♒ ♓

Beauty	Commit
Believe	Compassion
Believable	Complete
Bliss	Confidence
Breakdown	Content
Breathe	Control
Clarity	Conquer

Courage	Endure
Create	Enjoy
Desire	Escape
Dream	Family
Dreams	Faith
Drive	Fearless
Empower	Fighter

Focus	Happiness
Forgive	Happy
Freedom	Harmony
Glory	Honesty
Goodness	Honor
Grace	Hope
Gratitude	Humble

Imagine	Knowledge
Inspire	Laugh
Inspiring	Lead
Integrity	Leading
Joy	Learn
Joyful	Life
Kind	Live

Limitless	Overcome
Love	Passion
Loving	Patience
Mindful	Peace
Memories	Positive
Motivate	Power
Now	Powerful

Pride	Spirited
Safe	Strength
Satisfaction	Strong
Satisfy	Succeed
Saved	Success
Skill	Trust
Spirit	Trustworthy

Truth	Beauty
	Believe
Winner	Believable
	Bliss
Wisdom	Breakdown
	Breathe
Wise	Clarity
Worthy	Commit
	Compassion
Yes	Complete
I Love You	Confidence

Content	Enjoy
Control	Escape
Conquer	Family
Courage	Faith
Create	Fearless
Desire	Fighter
Dream	Focus
Dreams	Forgive
Drive	Freedom
Empower	Glory
Endure	Goodness

Grace	Inspiring
Gratitude	Integrity
Happiness	Joy
Happy	Joyful
Harmony	Kind
Honesty	Knowledge
Honor	Laugh
Hope	Lead
Humble	Leading
Imagine	Learn
Inspire	Life

Live	Peace
Limitless	Positive
Love	Power
Loving	Powerful
Mindful	Pride
Memories	Safe
Motivate	Satisfaction
Now	Satisfy
Overcome	Saved
Passion	Skill
Patience	Spirit

Spirited	Worthy
Strength	Yes
Strong	I Love You
Succeed	Beauty
Success	Believe
Trust	Believable
Trustworthy	Bliss
Truth	Breakdown
Winner	Breathe
Wisdom	Clarity
Wise	

Commit	Dream
Compassion	Dreams
Complete	Drive
Confidence	Empower
Content	Endure
Control	Enjoy
Conquer	Escape
Courage	Family
Create	Faith
Desire	Fearless

Fighter	Harmony
Focus	Honesty
Forgive	Honor
Freedom	Hope
Glory	Humble
Goodness	Imagine
Grace	Inspire
Gratitude	Inspiring
Happiness	Integrity
Happy	Joy

Joyful	Love
Kind	Loving
Knowledge	Mindful
Laugh	Memories
Lead	Motivate
Leading	Now
Learn	Overcome
Life	Passion
Live	Patience
Limitless	Peace

Positive	Spirited
Power	Strength
Powerful	Strong
Pride	Succeed
Safe	Success
Satisfaction	Trust
Satisfy	Trustworthy
Saved	Truth
Skill	Winner
Spirit	Wisdom

Wise

Worthy

Yes

I Love You

Emma

Olivia

Ava

Amelia

Isabella

Sophia

Charlotte

Kelly

Mia

Mila

Harper

Brittany

Evelyn

Marguerite

Luna

Abigail	Toni
Camila	Penelope
Aria	Carla
Ella	Layla
Elizabeth	Grace
Avery	Barbara
Emily	Nora
Victoria	Eleanor
Scarlett	Zoey
Sofia	Chloe

Nicole	Nicole
Nova	Hannah
Madison	Lillian
Riley	Emilia
Rachel	Cynthia
Everly	Addison
Stella	Hazel
Aurora	Darnell
Lily	Leah
Ellie	Violet

Zoe	Violet
Audrey	May
Gia	April
Bella	June
Natalie	Marie
Lisa	Maria
Willow	Genesis
Amanda	_____
Julia	**Emma**
Denise	**Olivia**

Ava	Marguerite
Amelia	Luna
Isabella	Abigail
Sophia	Camila
Charlotte	Aria
Kelly	Ella
Mia	Elizabeth
Mila	Avery
Harper	Emily
Brittany	Victoria
Evelyn	Scarlett

Sofia	Nicole
Toni	Nova
Penelope	Madison
Carla	Riley
Layla	Rachel
Grace	Everly
Barbara	Stella
Nora	Aurora
Eleanor	Lily
Zoey	Ellie
Chloe	Nicole

Hannah	Gia
Lillian	Bella
Emilia	Natalie
Cynthia	Lisa
Addison	Willow
Hazel	Amanda
Darnell	Julia
Leah	Denise
Violet	Violet
Zoe	May
Audrey	April

June	HENRY
Marie	ALEXANDER
Maria	SEBASTIAN
Genesis	MASON
	ETHAN
	LOGAN
---------	MICHAEL
LIAM	DANIEL
NOAH	JACOB
WILLIAM	JACKSON
OLIVER	MATEO
LUCAS	WYATT
BENJAMIN	SAMUEL
ELIJAH	OWEN
JAMES	JACK

JOHN	ISAAC
THEODORE	DYLAN
DAVID	LINCOLN
CARTER	ANTHONY
LEVI	GABRIEL
JOSEPH	JAYDEN
GRAYSON	EZRA
JULIAN	CALEB
AIDEN	ISAIAH
JAXON	ELIAS
ASHER	JOSIAH
MATTHEW	THOMAS
LEO	
HUDSON	_____
LUKE	

Liam	Ethan
Noah	Logan
William	Michael
Oliver	Daniel
Lucas	Jacob
Benjamin	Jackson
Elijah	Mateo
James	Wyatt
Henry	Samuel
Alexander	Owen
Sebastian	Jack
Mason	John

Theodore	Hudson
David	Luke
Carter	Isaac
Levi	Dylan
Joseph	Lincoln
Grayson	Anthony
Julian	Gabriel
Aiden	Jayden
Jaxon	Ezra
Asher	Caleb
Matthew	Isaiah
Leo	Elias

Josiah Thomas

Liam
Noah
William
Oliver
Lucas

Benjamin
Elijah
James
Henry
Alexander
Sebastian
Mason

Ethan	Wyatt
Logan	Samuel
Michael	Owen
Daniel	Jack
Jacob	John
Jackson	Theodore
Mateo	David

CARTER	ASHER
LEVI	MATTHEW
JOSEPH	LEO
GRAYSON	HUDSON
JULIAN	LUKE
AIDEN	ISAAC
JAXON	DYLAN

Lincoln

Anthony

Gabriel

Jayden

Ezra

Caleb

Isaiah

Elias

Josiah

Thomas

www.ingramcontent.com/pod-product-compliance
Lightning Source LLC
Chambersburg PA
CBHW080457220526
45465CB00006B/2300